A USER'S GUIDE TO THE OFFICIAL RECORDS OF THE AMERICAN CIVIL WAR

by

Alan C. and Barbara A. Aimone

Foreword

by

Herman Hattaway

White Mane Publishing Company, Inc.

This White Mane Publishing Company, Inc. publication
was printed by
Beidel Printing House, Inc.
63 West Burd Street
Shippensburg, PA 17257 USA

In respect for the scholarship contained herein, the acid-free paper used in this book meets the guidelines for permanence and durability of the Committee on Production Guidelines for Book Longevity of the Council on Library Resources.

For a complete list of available publications
please write
White Mane Publishing Company, Inc.
P.O. Box 152
Shippensburg, PA 17257 USA

Library of Congress Cataloging-in-Publication Data

Aimone, Alan Conrad, 1941-
A user's guide to the official records of the American Civil War / by Alan C. and Barbara A. Aimone ; foreword by Herman Hattaway.
p. cm.
Includes bibliographical references and indexes.
ISBN 0-942597-38-9 (alk. paper) : $12.00
1. United States--History--Civil War, 1861-1865--Sources. 2. United States. War Dept. The War of the Rebellion. 3. United States. War Dept. The official military atlas of the Civil War. 4. Official records of the Union and Confederate Navies in the War of Rebellion. I. Aimone, Barbara A., 1946- . II. Title.
E464.A35 1993
973.7--dc20 93-9261
CIP

PRINTED IN THE UNITED STATES OF AMERICA

DEDICATION

To Ralph Geoffrey Newman whose enthusiasm and knowledge encouraged Alan's interest in the Civil War.

Table of Contents

APPENDICES

Foreword

Every Civil War scholar and serious student of that conflict will be well advised to become familiar with this, Alan and Barbara Aimone's very helpful and informative book about the *Official Records* and how best to go about using them. The Aimones are ideally suited to produce this tool: he is the Chief of Special Collections at the United States Military Academy, West Point, and she has a scientific and teaching background. I think this book is quintessentially useful and so important, it seems unthinkable to me that any writer worth his or her salt who is at all interested in the Civil War would not want to have a personal copy and to make frequent reference to it.

As the Aimones themselves correctly observe, no research about the American Civil War can be complete without using the *Official Records.* It also is probable that no research on the topic *is likely* to be complete — and certainly could not be cast in as high a level of quality as otherwise would have been possible — without being aware of what the Aimones tell us about the *Records.* The problems, for which this book offers remedy, exist because the *Official Records* are massive, complex, cumbersome (at least in some respects), and relatively poorly indexed. Indeed, from the very first, the inadequate indexing has been evident to every serious user.

It may be helpful to recall certain underlying realities that prevailed when the Records initially were published. They were not tailored to the needs of the professional historian. The historical profession was, after all, then only in its infancy. At that time there was even a considerable degree of haziness over just who might (and ought to) be a military historian. Some American scholars believed (perhaps a disturbingly large number still believe) that there could not be any good military historians. The ostensible major reason for this was because on the one hand soldiers do not possess the qualifications of a trained researcher and writer of history, while on the other, civilians do not possess sufficient insight into military matters. The infant American Historical Association and the U.S. War Department practically had a running feud over just how projects like the compilation of the *Official Records* ought to be handled.

As ultimately they were processed, the Records were intended primarily as reading for veterans, and only secondarily as source material for those who might prepare narrations of the campaigns. Perhaps this was for the best, for as the project unfolded, it proved so much more expensive than expected that interest as well as financial support sometimes lagged. Only pressure from veterans' organizations stopped several efforts to abort the entire project. Interestingly, many of those same veterans, especially officer veterans, exerted strong influences (which were stifled) to supplement the surviving contemporary records with ex post facto additions. The veterans for the most part, both Northerners and Southerners, were delighted with the appearance of the printed volumes. They constituted by far the principal readers, and they tended to read only the volumes that touched upon the campaigns and battles in which they had participated.

It is of course a tragedy that so much pertinent Confederate material did not get included. The scholarly world owes, ironically enough, much to Federal Major General Henry W. Halleck who, while the war still was going on, did much to prevent the destruction of captured Rebel Records, and later spent much of his own personal fortune to see that they were properly preserved and eventually presented in published form. Still, it is to the credit of the United States government that it made use of the services of Marcus J. Wright who, over a long period of time, did an exemplary job as Federal Agent for the Collection of Confederate Records and gleaned copies of many documents from private hands.

From time to time, one hears about a possible supplement being prepared to accompany the *Official Records*. There are, of course, mountains of additional documents in the possession of the

National Archives. I myself not very long ago was tasked by the Louisiana State University Press to give an assessment of proposal for the preparation and publication of such a supplement. If one ever does appear, we shall hope that the Aimones are still around and will then prepare a new edition of this grand little book.

As to complete sets of the volumes being used by systematic researchers, not much happened for many decades after their initial publication. Possibly those critics were correct who denounced as wasteful the system which was used for distributing whole sets. One observer called the War Department's policy "bizarre," and suggested that during the 1880's and 1890's the books were haphazardly scattered "among individual officers and backwater posts where they were said to be propping open doors and windows." In any event, little good use was made of them by scholars, and in 1916 Professor Robert M. Johnston, then the leading American military historian, estimated that only five writers, one of them himself, had made *any* "intelligent" use of the series. It is equally bizarre that Matthew Forney Steele, who in 1909 published *American Campaigns* which was to prove a most important and long-used standard textbook, purposefully had stayed away from the *Official Records* out of fear that he "might yield to the temptation to read on, from one report to another, far beyond the time I have had to spare."

But as the historical profession grew, so too did the use of the *Official Records* by various scholars. At the same time use of them by professional military men increased: after 1912 the Army War College curriculum regularly included much technical investigation of Civil War campaigns and students made much use of the *Official Records* in preparing term papers. In the 1920's and 1930's Douglas Southall Freeman began to set the modern standard for the most judicious use of the *Official Records.* As he correctly demonstrated, they require internal and external analysis, and careful verification with a myriad of well selected other sources. The *Official Records* can, however, be of value to quite a few students other than those interested solely in military operations. To be sure, the Records *are primarily* military in nature, but they have been useful also to general historians, biographers, and poets and novelists. Investigators working in social history would be well advised to make use of this book.

The field of military history itself has undergone something of a transition, so much so that the term "new military history" has been coined. The field is identified by a broader-based construct, wherein psychological and social factors have come to be interlaced with more purely strategic, operational, or tactical narrative. The "new military historians" are, I suspect, going to find still more "new ways" to make good use of the *Official Records.*

HERMAN HATTAWAY

U.S. Military Academy at West Point
19 May 1991

ACKNOWLEDGEMENTS

We are indebted to many individuals and organizations for their encouragement, assistance and advice. The late Everett Beach Long and Joseph L. Eisendrath, Jr., as well as other members of the Chicago Civil War Round Table, stimulated and encouraged Alan's fascination with Civil War history, in general, and the *Official Records*, in particular. Without them, this volume would never have been tackled. We appreciate the efforts of several past and present National Archives staff members, Dallas Irvine (retired), Dale Floyd (now with the National Park Service), Mike Musick, Maryellen Trautman and Robert Gruber, who expeditiously answered questions, made suggestions and located sources. Anne Bailey, Georgia Southern College, shared her ideas for additional sources beyond the *Official Records.* The efforts of Charlotte Snyder and Paul Nergelovic, of the United States Military Academy Library, who located several elusive sources, are appreciated as is the assistance of Dean C. Allard, historian, Department of the Navy. We are grateful to Herman Hattaway, Visiting Military History Professor at West Point for his professional expertise, suggestions and editing.

INTRODUCTION

The United States Government achieved a landmark in historical publishing with the printing of *The War of the Rebellion: A Compilation of the Official Records of the Union and Confederate Armies*, (*Official Records, Armies; OR-Armies*). The 128 books have been heralded as "the single most valuable, most-quoted, and most sought-after source of the Civil War history," and "the most notable publication of its kind in America . . . or . . . the world."[1] Together with the *OR-Atlas* and the naval sequel, *The War of the Rebellion: A Compilation of the Official Records of the Union and Confederate Navies*, (*Official Records, Navies; OR-Navies*) those works have been used as major references for thousands of books and articles about the Civil War. Indeed, they serve as our key to understanding the Civil War; " . . . no other Civil War source is so rich or so voluminous . . ."[2] Those records ". . . present the battle as it was remembered by the principal actors weeks or at most several months after the event, before other kinds of literature had crowded in to give a different shape to memory and perception . . ."[3] It is impossible to research or write authoritatively about Civil War operations or personalities without consulting these monumental works. (*Official Records* or *Rebellion Records* will be used interchangeably when referring to both the *Official Records, Armies* and *Official Records, Navies* together.)

Though researchers have used the *Official Records* extensively throughout the years, many have not used them effectively — having fallen prey to the temptation of relying on them without critical evaluation or comparison with other sources. It is equally true that many historians, intimidated and overwhelmed by the sheer volume of information in the army and navy compilations, have under-used these valuable resources.

An understanding of the historical background, editorial policy, purpose and organization of the *Official Records* along with an understanding of the finding aids available will enable the researcher to locate, analyze and use the material they contain critically and appropriately, recognizing the need to balance the information gleaned from these records with that from other contemporary sources. The purpose of this monograph is to encourage the judicious use of the *Official Records* by providing an overview of the historical background along with a discussion of the selection and editorial policies that shaped the volumes. That information, in addition to a look at the strengths and limitations of the *Official Records*, will facilitate a balanced and effective approach to using these works.

CHAPTER I

Historical Background

General-in-Chief Henry Wager Halleck, in response to the difficulty he experienced writing his 1863 annual report advocated gathering and publishing Civil War official documents and reports. Prompted by Halleck, the Chairman of the Committee on Military Affairs, Republican Senator Henry Wilson of Massachusetts, introduced a Joint Resolution "to provide for the printing of the official reports of the armies of the United States." The Superintendent of Public Printing, Joseph Hutton Defrees, drafted a revised version of the resolution which called for printing of 10,000 copies of all significant Union military records related to the war and specified the records he chronologically arranged. Defrees' amended resolution, embraced by Wilson, was adopted by the House and Senate on May 19, 1864 and signed by President Abraham Lincoln the following day.[1]

Army Assistant Adjutant General Edward D. Townsend was charged with supervising work on the records, which began almost immediately. By the following summer, field reports of commanding officers were compiled into eight volumes and sent to Defrees for printing. Defrees, recognizing these books did not achieve the breadth of coverage anticipated, delayed their publication. It was obvious that Townsend was not the man for the job so Senator Wilson introduced a new resolution allocating funds to appoint an editor to oversee the compilation and printing of Union and Confederate military records.

Wilson estimated the project would cost no more than $500,000 and would be completed in about fifty volumes. Opponents in the Senate argued, prophetically, that costs could escalate to millions with the printing of as many as 500 volumes. Despite opposition, the new resolution which rescinded the original 1864 version, passed and was signed by President Andrew Johnson on July 27, 1866. The 1866 version required the Secretary of War to "appoint a competent person to arrange and prepare for publication the official documents relating to the rebellion" and develop a plan and cost estimate for the project within two years.[2] Peter J. Watson, former Assistant Secretary of War, was appointed to direct the project but never accepted or served.

The 1866 resolution in effect stopped the work in progress by the Adjutant General's Office — leaving about thirty volumes in various stages of completion. The whole project came to a halt for several years due to lack of funding and the government's need to concentrate on pressing reconstruction issues.

Union and Confederate veterans' organizations, miffed by that turn of events, lobbied both Congress and the Secretary of War to resume work on the Civil War records. Citizens felt the publication of the official records by the government would be a "guarantee of genuineness." Funds for the project were requested in the Secretary of War's annual reports from 1870-1873 but it was not until 1874

Lieutenant Colonel Robert N. Scott, editor of the *OR-Armies* from 1877-1887, established the editorial policies of the *Rebellion Records.*

U.S. National Archives and Records Service. *Prospectus: Military Operations of the Civil War: A Guide-Index to the "Official Records, Armies, 1861-1865."* Washington, D.C.: 1966

Congressman Henry Wilson proposed the bill to establish the "Official Records" project.

Wilson, Henry. *Military Measures of the United States Congress, 1861-1865.* New York: D. Van Nostrand, 1866

Major General Henry W. Halleck, Chief of Staff, promoted the concept of "Official Records."

Special Collections Division, U.S. Military Academy Library

TELEGRAMS RECEIVED

BY

MAJOR GEN. H. W. HALLECK,

WHILE

GENERAL-IN-CHIEF

AND

CHIEF OF STAFF.

VOLUME V.

THE PROPERTY OF THE UNITED STATES.

These reports are printed and bound for the uses of the War Department. They are not "publications," and are yet subject to revision—additions and rearrangement.

This volume is sent for safe-keeping to The Library at West Point

By order of the Secretary of War:

Robert N. Scott
Capt. 3d Art'y

Copy of the book plate identifying the preliminary printing of the *OR-Armies*. A set of the preliminary printings were sent by Lieutenant Colonel Scott to the U.S. Military Academy Library.

Special Collections Division, U.S. Military Academy Library

WASHINGTON:
WAR DEPARTMENT PRINTING OFFICE.
1877.

that Congress appropriated $15,000 to pay for publication of the Civil War records through Congressman James A. Garfield's amendment to an appropriations bill.[3] Garfield, in his amendment, was apparently the first to refer to these records as "the official records of the war of the rebellion." Townsend again was to be in charge of the publication.

The project, begun by Townsend a decade earlier, was back on track as Congress appropriated $90,000 in additional funding in 1875 and 1876. That funding was, however, still inadequate for the scope of the undertaking; Townsend had to ask his government clerks to work on the project during "non-official time" without pay.[4]

Though Townsend retired in 1875, work proceeded under a series of clerks who served as "superintendents" of the project. By December, 1877, forty-seven volumes of these *Reports of Military Operations During the Rebellion* were completed. Twenty "sample" copies of each were printed. Thirty-seven books contained Union papers while Confederate documents filled the remaining ten volumes. Material was printed chronologically. Since no attempt was made to organize material topically, readers would have to consult several volumes for information on one battle or incident.[5]

By late 1877, the Secretary of War, George W. McCrary, aware of the monumental scope of the project to publish Civil War records and the unwieldy and unsatisfactory result of the attempts to date, appointed a full-time curator to direct the staff of the "Publications Office, War Records," a new office established with the mission of organizing and publishing the Civil War official records.

Then-Captain Robert N. Scott, an aide to General Halleck during and after the Civil War, was appointed chief of this new office. Scott developed a plan to organize the records in a manner that would be useful for historical research and established criteria by which documents would be selected for inclusion. He supervised the completion of the initial 18 volumes, the first of which was distributed in July, 1881. He served as chief of the organization for ten years, until his death in March, 1887. In addition he is credited as the compiler of an additional 18 volumes (through Volume XXXVI) published after his death in recognition for his significant work on them.[6]

Captain Wyllys Lyman replaced Scott but left the position within four months when his health failed. He was replaced by Lieutenant Colonel Henry M. Lazelle who directed the publication of six volumes. Lazelle, dismissed when accused of allowing unauthenticated documents to be included in the *Official Records, Armies* was later exonerated by a Congressional committee. Congress, however, in response to the accusation, determined a three man Board of Publication, with a military president, should direct the remaining work. Major George B. Davis served as President of the first Board of Publication.

It was during Major Davis' Presidency that publication of the long awaited *Atlas* to accompany the *OR-Armies* was accomplished as sections appeared in serial form from 1891 to 1895. George B. Davis left the position in 1895 to become Professor of Law at West Point and was replaced by Major George W. Davis (no relation to George B. Davis) as President of the Board.

Work moved slowly under Major George W. Davis so Congress replaced him with Colonel Fred C. Ainsworth, who was also Chief of the Pension and Record Section in the Adjutant General's Office. Ainsworth reduced the staff of the War Records Office from 64 to 22 and assumed total control of the project by dissolving the Board of Publication. The War Records Office became the Publication Branch of the Record and Pension Office. He appointed Joseph W. Kirkley, one of the civilians on the original Board, to supervise the completion of the last 16 volumes. Kirkley had been involved with the project from inception to completion having been a clerk with the project under the Adjutant General's Office prior to 1878. Each volume had passed under his "personal examination."[7]

Publication of the *Official Records, Armies* was completed in 1901 when the *General Index* was printed. (A revised version of the *General Index* was printed in 1902.) The project had taken almost forty years from inception of the concept to its completion and cost over three million dollars.[8]

CHAPTER II

Obtaining the Records, Selection & Editorial Policies

The War of the Rebellion was the first conflict in which paper was used on a massive scale. The Federal bureaucracy required that every order, report, telegram and other communication be copied, transmitted, then recopied and retained.[1] The magnitude of the task of compiling the *Rebellion Records* can be appreciated when one realizes, "The papers examined were well-nigh beyond computation, being counted not by documents or boxes, but by tons, roomfuls or the contents of buildings. The volunteer records of discontinued commands (being the books and papers turned in by volunteer officers when mustered out) filled a large four-story warehouse; the Confederate records alone crowded an entire three-story building . . ."[2] Every document had to be read, evaluated, checked for duplication, and, if it was to be included, authenticated. As each document was processed, it was marked with a blue War Records Office stamp.

The 1877 appointment of Captain Robert N. Scott as Chief of the War Records Office, proved to be excellent for many reasons. His editorial policy and guidance would serve succeeding editors well. Scott brought with him both excellent credentials for the task and an overwhelming dedication to the job. As the aide-de-camp to Major General Halleck from 1863-1864 and again from 1867-1869, Scott was familiar with the military bureaucracy and the "records management" practices of various offices. His expertise on the various "ad-hoc" filing arrangements used by the Army often gave him valuable insight into where particular records would be found.[3]

Scott recognized the need to engage both former Union and Confederate officers in the editorial work. He believed that "absolute accuracy" would "only be secured by putting them (*OR-Armies*) in print under the immediate direction of those familiar with names of persons and places concerned, and with military terms, and who are zealously interested in this special work."[4] The ex-Confederate officers hired as editors assured impartiality in editing and publishing as did the fact that a "large percentage of the clerical staff" involved in the *OR-Armies* project was from the South. Between 1885 and 1897, an average of six officers and sixty-nine clerks toiled over the *Official Records, Armies* project.

Scott's first major challenge, as editor of the *OR-Armies*, was to establish editorial and document selection policies and develop a publication plan for the whole project. Scott quickly recognized the huge volume of material available would necessitate a consistent, critical selection policy. In general, Scott's criteria for documents to be included in the *OR-Armies* were quite simple: it had to be significant, official and produced during the war. Each of these criteria, while seemingly straight-forward, caused controversy and difficulty for the compilers. Scott was also acutely aware of the need to authenticate those documents that were included, especially when only copies were available to the War Records Office. This process required much time-consuming research and correspondence.

Determination of the significance of documents was quite subjective. Under that standard, editors would try to ascertain whether a particular document related to others and to a larger event. Scott was keenly aware of how difficult that process was. He wrote early in his tenure, "It is a matter of not small difficulty to decide upon what ought, or ought not, to appear in the publication of the War Records — even where, in matters of controversy, we have all of both, or more, sides of the question."[5]

The most controversial of the three selection criteria was the requirement that documents had to have been produced during the war. Scott vigorously extended that rule to mean without any correction of statements or alterations. He was convinced that unaltered documents would best serve veterans and historians who could more completely understand on what data (correct or not) war-time decisions were based. This policy created great controversy as many veterans wished to edit or "correct" their original papers and add "reminiscences." Scott, wary of the unreliability of human recollections, recognized, "If we were to accept post bellum reports from one [officer], we would have to extend the like privilege to others, and soon, we would be overwhelmed with controversial literature." Scott's arguments against allowing "corrections" or "amendments" persuaded Congress to defeat a bill introduced in 1882 that would provide for such "doctoring" of documents. Some annotation was allowed, however, as when individuals were vindicated of serious charges by post-war commissions.[6] In addition, editorial policy allowed for correction of bad grammar and misspellings.

The actual types of contemporary documents to be included were also defined and limited. Reports and orders that were already published were not included in the *OR-Armies.* Among these, the Adjutant General's Office published both *General Orders* and *Special Orders* while the Quartermaster's General published its own *General Orders*, as well as two large folios, *Commanders of the Army Corps, Divisions, and Brigades* and *Flags of the Army of the United States.* The Surgeon General's Office oversaw the publishing of its records and history, *Medical and Surgical History of the War of the Rebellion.* Among other published material left out of the *Official Records,*

Armies were reports of the Secretaries of War and Navy and the Joint Congressional Committee On the Conduct of the War. The routine letters of bureaus and departments, such as applications for appointments, arms, contracts, discharges, prisoner exchanges, muster rolls, charges of disloyalty, assorted claims and unsolicited advice or suggestions from individuals were also, thankfully, omitted. Material related to individuals, other than those of high rank was not included, either. Considering the scope of the selection process, the editors, in general, made wise decisions when choosing material to include in the *OR-Armies.*

The long arduous task of gathering Confederate material occupied much attention, time and effort. The first significant cache of Confederate material was collected when after the fall of Richmond, General Henry Wager Halleck ordered Confederate papers to be collected and sorted. Many significant rebel records had already been shipped away by the Confederate government when the fall of Richmond appeared imminent, while others were destroyed when the city was set ablaze. Halleck's Aide-de-Camp, Colonel Richard D. Cutts, did manage to ship "349 boxes, hogsheads, and barrels . . ." of Confederate papers to the Department of War in May.[7] Less than a month after President Abraham Lincoln's assassination, Halleck wrote to Secretary of War Edward M. Stanton regarding those Confederate papers, ". . . there may be found among them much evidence in regard to plots of assassination, incendiarism, treason, etc. . . . At any rate, they will prove of great value to those who may hereafter write the history of this great rebellion."[8]

Stanton quickly recognized the need for a separate bureau within the Adjutant General's office to oversee ". . . the collection, safekeeping, and publication of the Rebel Archives . . ."[9] Possibly at Halleck's suggestion, Stanton appointed Professor Francis Lieber, a Columbia College political scientist, to be in charge of the Confederate records.

In August, 1865, a total of 499 boxes and barrels of records as well as three wagon loads of mail were in Lieber's custody.[10] Stanton and Lieber both expected and hoped the documents would contain evidence linking Jefferson Davis to Lincoln's assassination.

". . . Lieber was tireless in his search for documents to connect Davis and his associates with the tragic event of April 14. This fruitless search overshadows all the others made by the Archives office during the first two years of its existence."[11]

Despite the lack of evidence to link Davis with the assassination plot or with the cruel treatment of Union prisoners, Lieber was convinced Davis' attitude was sufficient to condemn him.[12] Though Lieber was unable to gather acceptable evidence against Davis, he did succeed in overseeing the organization and classification of those captured records. Undoubtedly, the government's imprisonment of Jefferson Davis and Lieber's zealous search for incriminating evidence against Confederate leaders insured, however, that few private Southern papers would voluntarily be turned over to officials in Washington for some time to come.

Then almost a decade later, in 1875, former Confederate Brigadier General Marcus Joseph Wright offered a collection of Confederate reports to the Department of War in return for whatever that Department felt they were worth. It paid him $2,000. His offer to locate other Southern documents was not accepted, however. Undaunted, Wright asked for a list of the records already in the War Department's possession and set out to locate others. On July 1, 1878 Wright secured an appointment as "Agent of the War Department for the Collection of Confederate Records," charged with securing possession or use of "battle reports, correspondence, rolls, and returns and any matter relating to prisoners of war."[13]

Wright's first major success was to arrange, with Scott's approval, an agreement between the Southern Historical Society and the War Records Office for reciprocal free access to each other's Confederate documents. Prior to this time, the Society's offer to allow use of each other's Confederate documents was rejected by the War Records Office. Pleased with the War Records Office change of heart, and impressed with Agent Marcus Wright and other War Records Office personnel, the Society encouraged Southerners to share their manuscripts with that Federal agency "now under control and management which give assurance of fair play in both the compila-

Former Confederate Brigadier General Marcus J. Wright helped collect and organize Confederate papers in the *Rebellion Records.*

Irvine, Dallas D. "Archives Office of the War Department — Depository of Captured Confederate Archives, 1866-1881," *Military Affairs,* 10 (Spring, 1946), 107

Reverend William Jones, Secretary of the Confederate Historical Society, allowed Confederate documents to be included in the *Rebellion Records* project.

Jones, John William. *Christ in the Camp; Or, Religion in Lee's Army.* Richmond, VA: B. F. Johnson, 1887

tion and the publication of the 'official history of the war' . . ."[14] The Society even offered to "take charge" of manuscripts for Southerners while copies were made for both the Society and the War Records Office.[15]

From 1878 to 1917, Wright, and other ex-Confederate officers, traveled extensively throughout the Southern states locating significant Confederate records. Large numbers of documents were donated and others loaned so copies could be made in Washington. The families of many Confederate soldiers, however, thought of the Confederate documents in their possession as "heirlooms" and refused to part with them, even for copying. They were willing to make copies to send to Washington, though. Scott, in need of Confederate material, "had to accept as authentic much material that donators could have changed, either through error or a desire to 'correct' the original." The best the War Records Office could do in these cases was to require that donors certify, in writing, the authenticity of such copies.[16]

Despite all efforts to gather important official Confederate documents, that material still proved to be much scarcer than Union records; publication of the *Official Records, Army* had to proceed with significantly fewer Confederate than Union documents.

CHAPTER III

ORGANIZATION AND DISTRIBUTION OF THE *OR-ARMIES*

The *Official Records, Armies* are contained in 127 books plus a *General Index* and accompanying *Atlas.* Editor Robert N. Scott, recognizing the need to arrange the Rebellion Records topically (rather than in strict chronological order), designed a plan to divide the mass of material into four separate topical series.

By far the longest and most complex is Series I whose 53 volumes focus on military operations. As many of these volumes are printed in two to five separate "Parts," Series I totals 111 books. (Volume 12 is particularly unique; four books are required to publish its three parts as Part 2 contains a supplement.) Scott explained the organization of Series I: ". . . reports will be arranged according to campaigns and several theaters of operations (in the chronological order) and the Union reports of any event will be immediately followed by the Confederate accounts." . . . in the "correspondence, etc., not embraced in the reports proper, will follow . . ."[1] Simply stated, orders and reports relating to a battle or campaign are arranged to give a complete history of that event in the same volume. Union documents precede Confederate documents for each event while correspondence related to each operation follows the official reports. "The chief idea was to present to the reader in one volume a connected account of any military event both from Union and Confederate records . . ."[2] Though the plan was to separate official "reports" from correspondence, this separation was not always achieved. "One may search in vain through the correspondence for a desired letter — only to find it placed with the reports. On the other hand, many minor reports are treated as correspondence and are placed in different volumes from hundreds of similar dispatches."[3]

Each volume in Series II-IV is contained within one book. The eight volumes of Series II include Union and Confederate correspondence, orders, reports and returns concerning prisoners-of-war and political prisoners. Volume 8 of Series II is of particular interest. It contains documents relating to the most prominent post Civil War trials — that of Captain Henry Wirz, the infamous Commandant of the Andersonville Prison Camp and those of the conspirators in the Abraham Lincoln assassination plot.

The five volumes of Series III include "miscellaneous" Union correspondence and records largely pertaining to the organization and logistics of the Union war effort. Also to be found is correspondence between Union and Confederate authorities.

"Miscellaneous" records and correspondence of the Confederacy, including Acts passed by the Confederate States Congress, are found in the three volumes of Series IV. Other valuable material found in Series IV are the General and Special Orders of the Confederate States Army as well as correspondence relating to conscription and blockade running.

Researchers typically cite material in the *OR-Armies* by Series, Volume, Part (if applicable) and page. Beginning with the publication of Volume 26, the 36th book, the compilers added a Serial

Number to the spine of each book. (Reprintings list a Serial Number on all book spines.) Serial Numbers 112 and 113 were originally planned as indexes to Series I; though never published, those serial numbers were reserved, so there is a gap of two books between Serial Numbers 111 and 114.

The *General Index* published in 1901 (revised in 1902) purports to index the entire 127 books of text. It also includes a listing of the *OR-Armies* volumes and parts along with a synopsis of each volume. The 1902 revision contains "Additions and Corrections" to the version published in 1901. *General Index* citations are helpful (though cumbersome) in locating information in the text about people, places and units. (The *General Index* will be discussed at some length in the section on "Finding Aids.")

A series of laws passed from 1880 until 1904 controlled the distribution of the *OR-Armies.* The initial law, dated June 16, 1880, provided for the printing of 10,000 copies of the work. The law dated August 7, 1882 specified 11,000 copies were to be published. One thousand copies were allocated to executive departments while another 1,000 sets were to be distributed by the Secretary of War to Army officers and contributors. These two thousand sets were specially bound in half red Morocco for presentation to Civil War corps commanders and to members of Congress at the time of publication. Eight thousand three hundred copies were set aside for "such libraries, organizations and individuals" as designated by Senators, Representatives and Delegates of the Forty-Seventh Congress. (Each Senator could designate 26 recipients; Representatives and Delegates had 21 designees.) The remaining 700 sets were to be sold.

Besides the 11,000 *OR-Armies* sets authorized by the 1882 law, some 1,840 copies of each volume were printed to be bound as part of the Congressional serial set. These sets were used for members of Congress and distribution to government depository libraries.[4] These are included in the House Miscellaneous Documents. (Appendix VII provides a chart correlating House Miscellaneous Documents and Serial numbers with the War and Navy Department designations for each book in the *OR-Armies* and *OR-Navies.*)

An accurate count of the complete sets distributed is impossible to determine, incomplete sets accumulated over the years as libraries and organizations originally designated to receive the compilation "became extinct."[5]

In an attempt to distribute the remaining incomplete sets, an act dated March 3, 1903 allowed each Member of Congress to name two libraries or educational institutions to receive a set. In addition, each Congressman was allocated a complete set for his own use. The law allowed for additional copies to be printed and bound to complete the sets distributed under this law.

This law did not, however, achieve its full purpose. In a 1920 letter to President Woodrow Wilson, Secretary Newton Baker reported that approximately 62 Congressmen failed to make their designations. The Adjutant General's Office was storing 36,551 volumes of the *OR-Armies* of which 197 complete sets could be made. "The remaining 11,244 volumes are practically valueless . . ." Complete sets could no longer be made; the printing plates were destroyed under the 1903 Act.[6]

CHAPTER IV

OR-ATLAS

The long awaited *Atlas to Accompany the Official Records of the Union and Confederate Armies (Atlas)* began to take form when First Lieutenant Calvin Duvall Cowles, an 1873 West Point graduate, joined the War Records Office early in 1889. He found some 772 maps already in the files. Cowles, obviously underestimating the scope of the *Atlas* project, wrote to Lieutenant Colonel Henry M. Lazelle, then editor of the *OR-Armies*, "I think it is safe to say that about four hundred maps will be required for the *Atlas*, in addition to those appearing in the volumes. Allowing an average of four maps to a plate, one hundred plates or sets of plates would be required."[1]

In contrast, the *Atlas*, as completed six years later, reproduced 821 maps, 106 engravings and 209 drawings. The 178 double-page plates contain not only maps of varying sizes and scale but also cartographic sketches, fortification plans, hand-drawn and photographic landscape views, as well as sketches of equipment, uniforms, weapons, badges, buttons and flags.

The Atlas is divided into four sections:

1. Plates 1-135C (a total of 138 plates) — Military Operations in the Field
2. Plates 136-161 — The General Topographic Map
3. Plates 162-171 — Military Divisions and Departments
4. Plates 172-175 — Miscellaneous (includes drawings of uniforms, equiment, flags and insignia)

By far the largest number of maps relate, as expected, to military operations. They are contained on Plates 1-135C in Section I. Designed to be used in conjunction with the text of Series I of the *OR-Armies*, these maps and other illustrative materials are arranged in a general chronological order. Exceptions to this arrangement are numerous, however. Maps and sketches were rearranged to fit together "economically" on a plate. Also, in general, maps an officer submitted with his report were kept in close proximity although they may have spanned a fairly long time frame. In addition, some maps were obtained too late to be included in their proper sequence and were placed further back in the Atlas.

Most of the illustrative material in the first section of the *Atlas* were attachments to reports printed in the *OR-Armies* and were drawn by engineers, draftsmen and, on occasion, general officers. Those illustrations were primarily after-action maps or sketches prepared to accompany reports. Other maps included were those found in War Department files and a few prepared during post-war battlefield remapping projects. Actual maps used during battle are quite rare; two significant examples of ones that were are General Philip Henry Sheridan's map of Perryville and General William Tecumseh Sherman's Shiloh map. In addition, hand-drawn landscape views are reproduced on Plates 121-130.

The maps, plans and views contained in Section I of the *Atlas* are referenced in different ways in the *OR-Armies* reports they illustrate. In books completed before the *Atlas* was prepared, footnotes to maps read "To appear in the *Atlas.*" Early *OR-Armies* volumes contain some footnotes to graphic material stating "Not found." If the missing map was later found and included in the *Atlas*, the map includes a reverse citation indicating the volume and page number where associated material is located in the *OR-Armies*. It was not until Volume 43, Part 1 (Serial Number 90) of the *OR-Armies* that footnotes refer the user to the specific *Atlas* plate and map number where the illustration to accompany a report can be found.

Despite the seemingly large number of "battle" maps reproduced in the *Atlas* and in other sources, there was a serious dearth during the Civil War of decent "war zone" maps for planning campaigns and maneuvers, a fact lamented by both Union and Confederate officers. Union Colonel Theodore Lyman wrote of the "uselessness" of the maps furnished to the staff of the Army of the Potomac previous to the campaign of May, 1864, while Confederate Brigadier General Richard Taylor stated, ". . . we were profoundly ignorant of the country, were without maps, sketches or proper guides . . ."[2] In the years prior to the Civil War, Topographical Engineers did an excellent job mapping the far west, the nation's boundaries and the Great Lakes but no effort had been made to map the south. The exception was that accurate maps were available for coastal areas because the Coast and Geodetic Survey had completed mapping the Atlantic and Gulf Coasts prior to the Civil War.

Though neither side could boast an abundance of accurate maps from which to plan strategy during most of the war, the map situation for the Union improved as the war progressed and the number of topographers expanded. Before war's end, the Topographical Corps (merged during the war into the Corps of Engineers) included 105 officers, 752 enlisted men and an unknown number of civilians. The Confederacy suffered more as they lacked a corps of trained topographers to prepare maps. They also lacked paper, drafting supplies and even ink to reproduce the maps they had. There is also evidence that, for security reasons, the Confederacy chose to supply

Officer of the 153rd New York Volunteer Infantry Regiment in his tent and field office.
Poe Civil War Collection, Special Collections Division, U.S. Military Academy Library

Telegraph wagons, attached to field headquarters provided a vital communication link between military and civilian leaders. Telegrams were often the first reports of the Civil War. Millions of battle related telegrams were sent during the Civil War; thousands are included in the *Rebellion Records*.
Poe Civil War Collection, Special Collections Division, U.S. Military Academy Library

Shelves of Confederate records in temporary storage during the editorial stages of the *OR-Armies*.
Irvine, Dallas D. "Archives Office of the War Department — Depository of Captured Confederate Archives, 1866-1881," *Military Affairs*, 10 (Spring, 1946), 107

only the commanding general and corps commanders with complete area maps. This presumably lessened the chance that maps, which might prove useful to the Union, could be captured.[3]

Moreover, most of the Confederate maps that were in existence were apparently lost or destroyed. When Richmond fell, Captain Albert H. Campbell, Cartographer of the Army of Northern Virginia, placed his maps on an archives train bound for Raleigh, North Carolina. The train was burned and the original maps "lost." The fate of these maps was never definitely determined though Campbell reported, "It is supposed [the box or two containing the maps] was burned with the train, or pillaged, for fragments of some of the maps were reported to have been seen along that route in North Carolina." Campbell reported that although some worthless securities that were with the maps were returned to him 19 years later, he never received the maps or letters. The negatives of his maps reportedly met a fiery end after Campbell entrusted them to his private secretary to carry to Macon, Georgia. The secretary indicated he hid the negatives in a lady's trunk on his return trip to Richmond but when he learned the baggage of returning fugitives was to be examined, he burned the negatives.[4]

For all these reasons, Confederate maps were scarce when the *Atlas* was compiled — fewer than one fourth of the maps are of Confederate origin, though a Confederate map for each major operation or battle is included. Of those Confederate maps that were reproduced there, over one-half were prepared by Major Jedediah Hotchkiss, the Chief Topographer of the Army of Northern Virginia. Cowles, in fact, consulted Hotchkiss during preparation of the *Atlas.*[5]

The second section of the *Atlas* — Plates 136-161 — is a "General Topographic Map" of the entire theater of the war. This, however, is far from complete; less than half the locations and geographic features referred to in the names of operations are included and only about two-thirds of those places actually indexed in the *Atlas* are noted on the topographic map plates.

The third section of the *Atlas*, "Military Divisions and Departments" is contained on Plates 162-171. On a base map of the United States, the names and boundaries of Union and Confederate com-

Union Cavalry Generals Wesley Merritt, Philip Henry Sheridan, George Crook, David McMurtrie Gregg and George Armstrong Custer studying a campaign map.
Poe Civil War Collection, Special Collections Division, U.S. Military Academy Library

Lieutenant Daniel Cowles, compiler of the *OR-Atlas*, here pictured as a U.S. Military Academy cadet in 1871.
Cullum File No. 2492, Special Collections Division, U.S. Military Academy Library

General William T. Sherman sketched his own campaign maps.
Poe Civil War Collection, Special Collections Division, U.S. Military Academy Library

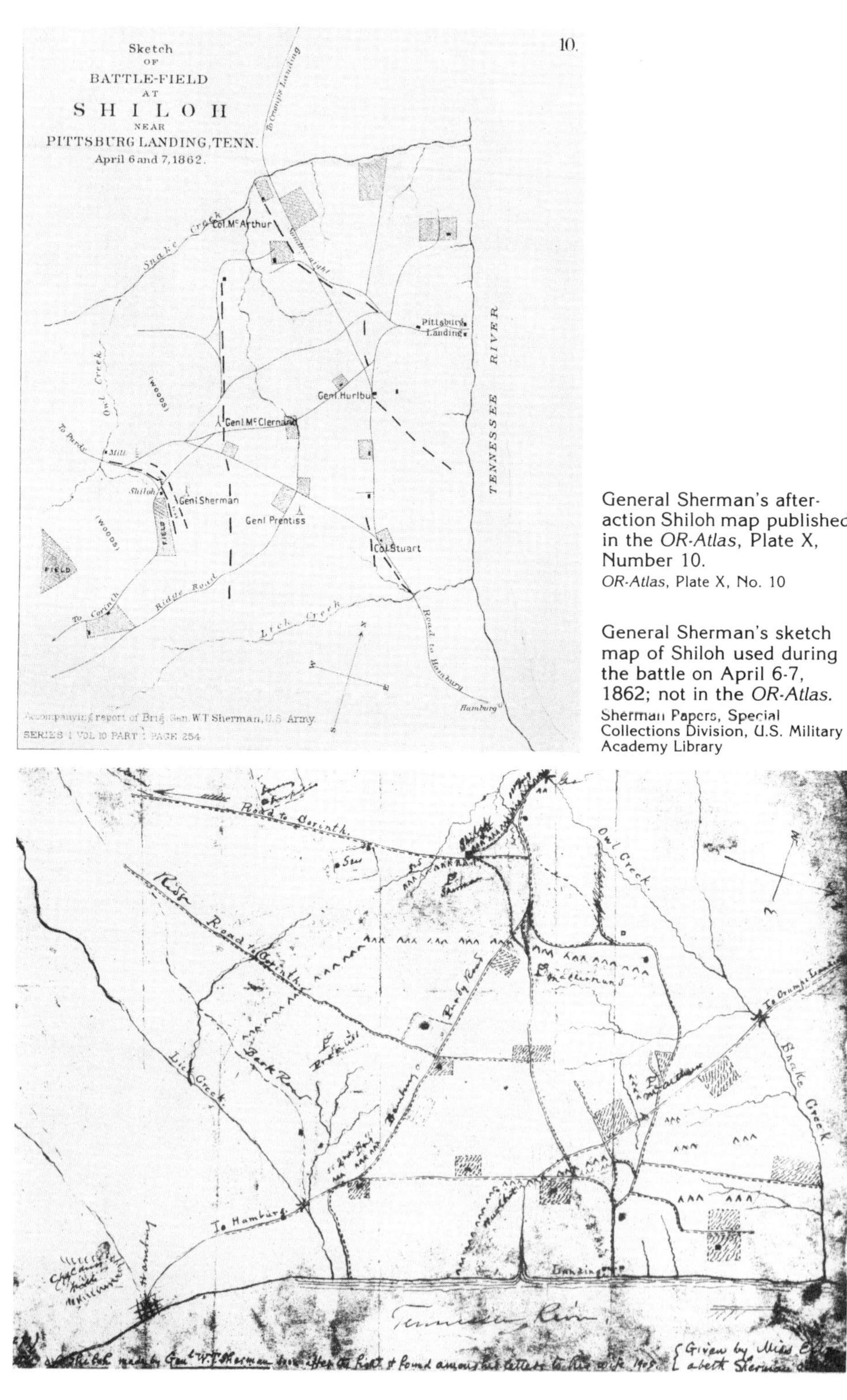

General Sherman's after-action Shiloh map published in the *OR-Atlas*, Plate X, Number 10.
OR-Atlas, Plate X, No. 10

General Sherman's sketch map of Shiloh used during the battle on April 6-7, 1862; not in the *OR-Atlas.*
Sherman Papers, Special Collections Division, U.S. Military Academy Library

mands are shown as are military departments and divisions. The maps trace the changes in these boundaries and departments throughout the war. The first map shows the situation for December 31, 1860, while subsequent maps show Union and Confederate boundaries on June 30 and December 31 each year during the war. The last map depicts the status on April 9, 1865.

Section IV of the *Atlas*, simply designated "Miscellaneous," consists of four plates (172-175) with sketches of equipment, uniforms, insignia of rank, flags and badges; uniforms and flags are shown in color.

In preparing the maps for printing, Cowles used color to identify Union and Confederate lines and to emphasize topographic features. In Section I, Federal positions are in dark blue while red depicts Confederate lines. Elevations are highlighted with brown. A light shade of blue indicates narrow bodies of water while major waterways are a slightly "muddy" green. Light green outlines areas of vegetation.

Julius Bien and Company of New York City, a highly respected and skilled lithographer and printer engraved and printed the *OR-Atlas*. Bien's government mapping work began when Secretary of War, Jefferson Davis, awarded him a contract to make maps for the Pacific Railroad surveys in the 1850's. His connection with the United States government continued during the war as he equipped the field map printing office that Major General William T. Sherman took on his march to the sea.[6]

The *Atlas* plates were originally published in 38 separate paper covered folios, most containing five plates each. (The exceptions were the folios containing the Table of Contents and Indexes and the three plate folio for Plates 135 A, B and C.) The first three folios were ready in 1891; the entire *Atlas* was complete in 1895.

Sets were distributed at no charge to essentially the same people and institutions who received a complimentary copy of the *OR-Armies*. Unissued copies were authorized to be sold. The typical five plate folio cost 40 cents while the whole unbound series of 138 plates and indexes, etc. sold for $14.50. As a more durable alternative to the folio sets, the *Atlas* was offered for sale as two or three bound books available in either a red or brown "half-turkey morocco" binding at a cost of $22.50 and $26.50 respectively.[7]

Though there are many errors in the maps reproduced in the *Atlas*, and scales, particularly verbal scales [*i.e.* 1 inch = 1 mile], are not accurate, it is of great value to the Civil War historian. The contemporaneous maps actually used in military operations, or drawn for reports shortly after battle, reveal what commanders knew and, equally significant, did not know, of the topography of the area in which they were fighting or moving. "They starkly reveal the misapprehensions that handicapped generals groping through strange and often dangerous country." The maps ranging "From rough sketches to cartographic masterpieces . . . graphically portray the course of the Civil War — as it actually went and as the men who waged it thought it went or hoped it would go."[8]

Confederate States' Ram Atlanta. OR-Navies editors made special efforts to include a number of photographs or drawings of Civil War vessels.

NOR, Series I, Volume 14

CHAPTER V

HISTORICAL BACKGROUND AND ORGANIZATION OF THE *OR-NAVIES*

The thirty-one volume *Official Records, Navies* is the most quoted source in Civil War naval studies. Naval Civil War Official Records are of particular importance and value. They chronicle the first major conflict in which steam powered vessels were heavily used and in which rams, torpedoes, iron clads, and rifled ordnance "revolutionized the art of naval warfare."[1] It is also a valuable, though often overlooked, resource for students of army operations. The impact of naval support on army campaigns was often significant. The researcher, failing to recognize the importance of naval contributions will also fail to completely understand the campaigns. Not to be forgotten, either, is the historically valuable cache of Confederate diplomatic papers in Series II of the *OR-Navies.*

The *Official Records, Navies* was undertaken almost as an afterthought. The publication of the *OR-Armies* in 1881 motivated the Navy, wanting of course not to be outdone by the Army, to convince Congress to appropriate funds to collect, compile and arrange naval records of the War of the Rebellion. Congress did so on July 7, 1884.

Professor James R. Soley initiated the *OR-Navies* publication and continued to support the project as an Assistant Secretary of the Navy.
"The Assistant Secretary of the Navy," *Harper's Weekly* (vol. 34, no. 1755, August 9, 1890)

Prior to the appropriation, Chief of the Bureau of Navigation, Captain John Grimes Walker, had already begun gathering naval records. The 1884 Act, however, provided $2,640 for a clerk and two copyists to work on the compilation under the newly formed "Office of Library and Naval War Records."

The new office was headed by Professor James Russell Soley, United States Navy, who had been serving as officer-in-charge of the Bureau of Navigation's departmental library since 1882. Soley, who had been a professor of history and law at the U.S. Naval Academy, lent "vigor and direction" to the editing.[2] He managed to acquire additional space for a "records office" where copying and preparation of material for publication progressed. The Office of the Chief of Naval War Records stamped "C.N.W.R." in red ink on naval documents copied for the *OR-Navies.* Those documents not copied were marked with a zero.[3]

In 1888 Congress appropriated funds for six additional clerks to work on the project. When appointed Assistant Secretary of the Navy in 1889, Soley left the helm of the Navy War Records project to a succession of five officers-in-charge but continued to actively lend support to the endeavor from his new position. "By fortunate coincidence," the Office of Library and Naval War Records was placed under the Secretary of the Navy's Office (from the Bureau of Navigation) and the officer-in-charge designated "Superintendent, Naval War Records." In 1890, the staff assigned to work on the Naval War Records increased to fourteen clerks.[4]

Lieutenant-Commander Frederick M. Wise, Jr. succeeded Soley as head of the Naval War Records project and, in turn, was replaced by Lieutenant-Commander Richard Rush in 1893 when Wise received orders to sea. It was under Rush's administration that the first volumes were published. In 1897, when Rush was assigned to sea duty, Professor Edward K. Rawson became superintendent of the *OR-Navies* project. Volumes 6-14 were published under his supervision. Mr. Charles W. Stewart succeeded Rawson in 1902 when Rawson was assigned to the U.S. Naval Academy. Stewart oversaw the completion of Series I (Volumes 15-27) as he remained with the Naval War Records Office until 1917. Work on the *OR-Navies*, including the publication of the three volumes of Series II, continued under the direction of Captain Charles C. Marsh who took over the helm in 1921.

Not surprisingly, as compilation of records proceeded, Confederate material proved elusive. Rawson's 1901 report revealed the limited success of an agent to seek out Civil War naval records: "The agent appointed by Congress has continued his inquiries, especially for Confederate material, of which there is little to be obtained, the greater part of the official documents having been destroyed at the close of the war. He has interested many people to make search for such papers as are pertinent for publication."[5]

One significant collection of Confederate documents that were obtained and included in the *OR-Navies* are the "Pickett Papers," the Confederate State Department Archives. That collection was named after Colonel John T. Pickett, a Confederate diplomat and Chief of Staff to Major General John Cabell Breckenridge. He was hired by the Confederate State Department Clerk, William J. Bromwell, to serve as his agent to negotiate the sale of these significant papers. Bromwell had gained possession of the papers when the Secretary of State, Judah B. Benjamin, entrusted the valuable documents to him when the Confederacy fell. Bromwell, for obvious reasons, remained anonymous throughout the negotiations.[6] These manuscripts, purchased in 1872 for $75,000, are found in Series II, Volume 3 of the naval compilation. "Embracing the larger part of the diplomatic correspondence of the Confederate Government, they have a far greater value than any of the collections of military papers or records."[7] Everett Beach Long, noted Civil War historian, considered the Pickett Papers ". . . the best available printed source of Confederate State Department correspondence . . ." They reveal much about Confederate foreign relations and purchasing operations.[8]

The first volume of the *Official Records, Navies* was published in 1894; volumes were printed regularly until 1917 when the 27 volumes of Series I were completed. Printing was then suspended until after World War I. The three volumes of Series II, published in 1921 and 1922, completed the thirty textual volumes of the *Official Records, Navies.*

The organization of the *OR-Navies* is simpler than its army counterpart. Divided into two series, the 27 volumes of Series I reproduced official reports, documents, etc. relating to both Union and Confederate naval operations. Volumes 1-3 follow, chronologically, the operations of cruisers on the high seas throughout the war. The remaining volumes concern Union and Confederate naval operations on the rivers and the Atlantic and Gulf Coasts. Operations are arranged by geographic region, "South Atlantic Blockading Squadron," "East Gulf Squadron," "Potomac and Rappahannock Rivers" and then subdivided chronologically.

The three volumes of Series II cover a variety of material. Volume 1 is divided into four parts: "Statistical Data of Union and Confederate ships," "Muster Rolls of Confederate Government Vessels," "Letters of Marque and Reprisal," and "Confederate Departmental Investigations, etc." Volume 2, "Navy Departmental Correspondence, 1861-1865" contains "Confederate Navy Correspondence." "Proclamations, Appointments, etc. of President Davis" and "State Department Correspondence with Diplomatic Agents, etc." can be found in Volume 3. Unsuccessful diplomatic efforts of the Confederacy to secure foreign recognition as a separate nation are documented in this volume.

Although the navy compilation lacks a separate atlas, most volumes covering the fields of operations do contain maps, tables, photographs, plans and sketches. "The insertion of accurate pictures [including drawings] of Union and Confederate naval vessels of war" was considered to be an important feature of the publication.[9]

CHAPTER VI

FINDING AIDS

The 147,668 pages of text in the *OR-Navies* and *OR-Armies* combined and the 1,136 maps and sketches in the *Atlas* quickly teach the researcher that finding aids are essential if relevant material in the volumes is to be located in a reasonable amount of time. A variety of finding aids were included in the *OR-Armies*, *OR-Navies* and the *Atlas* themselves. In addition, one modern in-depth finding aid, the *Guide-Index* published by the National Archives is available to the serious researcher.

OR-ARMIES FINDING AIDS

Effective, efficient use of a work as monumental and complex as the *OR-Armies* necessitates excellent indexing. Unfortunately, indexing of the *OR-Armies* fell well short of that ideal. Renowned Civil War historians, Bruce Catton and Allan Nevins stated, "Not least among the difficulties of using the work stands the wretched indexing."[1]

The original intent of the *OR-Armies* editors was to provide a two volume index (Serial Numbers 112 and 113) dedicated to just the complex 111 books of Series I. Those two index volumes never materialized, however. The one volume "comprehensive" *General Index* published in 1901 (revised in 1902) was an "abrupt change of plan."[2] It attempted to index the entire *OR-Armies* and, in effect, condensed into 1,087 pages some 11,563 pages of book indexes found throughout the compilation. Even when used in conjunction with the book indexes, it is inadequate, frustrating and time-consuming.

The 180,000 entries in the *General Index* include listings for people, places and military units only, not subjects. The citations only direct the user to Series and Volumes — no pages or even parts of multipart volumes are provided. Book indexes must then, in turn, be consulted.

The book indexes, too, have serious limitations — being ". . . full of gaps, and inadequate and erratic even for the subjects covered."[3] They do, however, include listings for subjects as well as those for people, places and military units. In addition, beginning with Volume V, book indexes cite, under the heading "Sketches," illustrations in that book.

A major flaw in the book indexes which make them time consuming to use is their failure to cite page references for sub-operations. Instead, they note only the officers whose reports on the overall operation should be consulted. The researcher must then look up the officers under the citation for the larger operation. Page references for the officers' reports, of course, cite only the beginning page of what may be a multi-page report so the researcher must scan the whole document to find information about the sub-operation being studied.

A further flaw in the indexing of the *OR-Armies* is the failure to index completely Trans-Mississippi locations. One attempt to fill that void is the *Index to Place Names Mentioned . . .*, a recent guide to the *OR-Armies* for the state of Louisiana.[4]

In addition to the indexes, the editors of the *Official Records, Armies* made other attempts at providing users with rudimentary finding aids. For Series I, a listing of the "Contents of Preceding Volumes" is printed at the beginning of each volume (beginning with Volume II, of course) and a "Summary of Principal Events" is found at the beginning of each chapter. That "Summary" lists events in the same chronological order as the reports covering the events are printed. Unfortunately, the actual page where each report begins is not included. In addition, the "Summaries" list some operations and events not documented in the text by reports without indicating that reports about these are not be found in the chapter.

A listing of "Reports" follows the "Summary of Principal Events" for each chapter. They are listed in the order in which they are published but again specific page references are absent. There is also no distinction there between Union and Confederate reports so the researcher cannot tell which is which.[5]

The compilers of the *Official Records, Armies* apparently came to recognize that listings of alternate unit names would be a valuable aid to users. Beginning with Volume 22, therefore, an alphabetical listing of "Alternate Designations of Organizations Mentioned in this Volume" precedes each book index. That helps users of *OR-Armies* locate relevant reports that might otherwise be overlooked if only the official unit designation, not the commanders' names associated with the unit, are known.

OR-ATLAS FINDING AIDS

Included within the *Atlas*, are finding aids to the maps reproduced in that volume, as well as to the illustrations in the *OR-Armies*.

The index to the *Atlas* is the most significant and useful finding aid provided to the *Atlas*. Place names and subjects, listed alphabetically, are accompanied by references to the *Atlas* plate and map numbers. In addition, under each state in the theater of operations is a listing of maps and subjects related to that state. Though generally accurate and fairly complete, this index is not consistently cross-referenced. In addition, citations to maps covering large areas do not include grid coordinates that could direct the user to the part of the map where that specific location is to be found.

The second useful finding aid in the *Atlas* is the "Table of Contents" which lists the plates in numerical order and provides a brief description of the maps and sketches contained on each plate. The dates associated with each map are indicated when appropriate.

Four additional internal finding aids are available. A "Listing of Maps, ETC., Contained In the Atlas" that correlate to the reports in the *OR-Armies* (through Volume 50) is provided in the front matter of the *Atlas.* The *Atlas* also provides a useful index to the maps and sketches in the *Or-Armies.* Listed alphabetically by geographic name or subject, each citation specifies the volume, part and page where the illustration can be found in the *OR-Armies.* Two directories of "Authorities" are included in the *Atlas* as well. One enumerates the people or organizations responsible for each illustration in the *Atlas,* along with the plate and map number. The other lists the "Authorities" credited for the maps and sketches in the *OR-Armies* and indicates the volume, part and page number where each is found.

The Newberry Library prepared a modern finding aid for maps in the *Atlas.* Its *Civil War Maps: A Graphic Index to the Atlas to Accompany the Official Records of the Union and Confederate Armies* is available for purchase through their bookstore. On modern state maps, arranged alphabetically, the graphic index outlines or highlights the area covered by maps in the *Atlas,* along with the plate and map number for each. That provides an alternate, though incomplete, index to *Atlas* maps when the modern map location of the area being studied is known. No fortification plans or landscape views are included in this graphic index, however.[6]

OR-NAVIES FINDING AIDS

Both a *General Index* and individual book indexes are included as major finding aids to the material in the *OR-Navies.* As the Naval Records project evolved, it became apparent that an "indexer" would be an asset to the staff; in 1907 that position was created, as was a "proof-reader" position.[7] The *General Index* was published in 1927 and quickly was recognized as a major reference source, not only as a finding aid to the 30 textual volumes of the *OR-Navies* but also as a "valuable guide to the spelling of names and places."[8]

The *OR-Navies, General Index* is the same as the *OR-Armies* in that the *General Index* volume does not contain page citations but refers the user to the series and volume where information on the topic can be found. The indexes of the individual volumes must then be used to determine the pages where the specific information is located. Indexes include citations to names of people, ships and naval battles.

In addition to the indexes, other finding aids are included in the *OR-Navies.* All volumes begin with enumeration of the "Contents of Preceding Volumes" and contain a "List of Illustrations" in the volume. The 27 volumes of Series I include an overall outline of the entire series as the "Order of Compilation of Naval War Records — Series I." "The Table of Contents" for each volume chronologically lists reports about principal events covered in the volume and indicates the pages where each report is found. Each book of Series I also contains a list of "U.S. Vessels of War . . ." mentioned in that particular volume, along with the vessels "rate," tonnage, class and number of guns. (As no page references are included in the "vessel" lists, however, the volume indexes must be consulted.)

The finding aids included in each of the three volumes of Series II vary as the types of reports and data vary significantly from volume to volume. In general, however, each section does begin with a useful "index" or "listing" of the contents in that section. Some of these "listings" include specific page references while others do not.

OFFICIAL RECORDS — GUIDE-INDEX AS A FINDING AID

The *Military Operations of the Civil War: A Guide-Index to the Official Records of the Union and Confederate Armies, 1861-1865 (Guide-Index)* is a valuable finding aid prepared by the National Archives and Records Service (more recently the National Archives Records Administration) "to remedy some of the deficiencies of the original indexing and to correct some of the errors and shortcomings of the original War Department official records compilation itself."[9] While it was clear that a complete re-indexing of the *OR-Armies* was not feasible, Dallas Irvine, Senior Military Specialist in the National Archives during the Civil War Centennial, conceived, proposed and outlined the multi-volume finding aid for the *"Rebellion Records"* which he believed was within the scope of the National Archives capability and which would facilitate research.

The serious researcher who hopes to thoroughly utilize all pertinent material in the *"Rebellion Records"* must consult the *Guide-Index.* Because the *Guide-Index* is a detailed, multi-faceted work, much time must be spent studying its content and organization before it can be effectively used.

The 5 volume, 9 part *Guide-Index* itself was fourteen years in the making. The "Prospectus," outlining the proposed contents and containing an introduction to the work, was published in 1966; publication date of the final volume (V) was 1980. The complete series is currently available only on microfilm. A condensed version (also out of print) was published in 9 booklets.

A particularly useful aspect of the *Guide-Index* is that it cross-references material in the *OR-Armies*, *OR-Navies* and the *Atlas.* This minimizes the possibility of the researcher overlooking pertinent data contained in those three sources. Furthermore, it was done by trained archivists who were not only familiar with Civil War records but also the needs of historical researchers. Thus the narrative provides search strategies including suggestions for other published sources to be used when material on the subject is lacking in the *Official Records.*

CHAPTER VII

VALUE OF THE *OR-ARMIES* AND *OR-NAVIES*

The value of the *Rebellion Records* to the student of the Civil War cannot be overestimated. They historically have been and continue to be, by far, the most complete, accessible, unbiased documentation of the War of the Rebellion. The prolific writings about and the continued interest in the American Civil War can, to a large measure, be attributed to the existence and widespread availability of the *Official Records.* The thousands of pages of text contained in the *OR-Armies* and *OR-Navies* combined make them a gold mine of information — much of it yet to be fully unearthed, sifted, analyzed and refined. The researcher who uses them effectively finds they provide a framework for the study of almost any Civil War related topic —

battles, campaigns, naval operations, unit histories, biographies and a myriad of other specialized military and civilian subjects. In fact, no research in that era can be complete without using the *Official Records.*

The editorial policy mandating only documents written during the war would be published in the *Rebellion Records* has proven to be an astute decision both historically and politically. From the historian's point of view, the *Official Records* are valuable tools; the correspondence and reports of the key players in the Civil War were reproduced without editing for accuracy or "retrospection." They reveal the information and misinformation available to the leaders as well as their knowledge and understanding of the situation at the time of the action. They reflect the intelligence available to leaders at that moment — intelligence that often was inaccurate or incomplete but on which actions were based. Because both Union and Confederate papers relating to the same event were published with no attempt at correction, the astute researcher can often gain insight into the whys and wherefores of the military decisions that shaped the outcome of individual battles, maneuvers and movements — and ultimately the war.

Politically, the editorial policy to include only contemporary material without correction allowed both Union and Confederate veterans to praise the *Rebellion Records* as an accurate, fair and complete history of the conflict. There has never been any significant questioning of the authenticity of the vast majority of the material published in the *Rebellion Records.* In fact, from the time the first long awaited volume of the *OR-Armies* was published, veterans of both sides, relied on them as they wrote their memoirs and reminiscences.

In some respects, an officer's correspondence can be more useful and revealing than his official reports and certainly should not be overlooked. It was often more candid, written without an eye to its preservation for posterity. The officer's assessment and comments were often less self-serving than in their official reports. Often, too, correspondence gives a deeper insight into personality and therefore may be of greater value in biographical studies.

The *Rebellion Records* contain, in addition to a vast amount of military documentation, a ". . . wealth of valuable material, of civil rather than military interest . . ."[1] This material, found primarily in Series II and IV of the *OR-Armies* and Series II of the *OR-Navies*, sadly, is underutilized by social, civil and political historians. The overwhelming emphasis on military operations in the *Rebellion Records* has, apparently, dissuaded those specialists from consulting those valuable sources. Indeed, even the formal titles of the two series specify they are the *Rebellion Records* of the armies and navies with no mention of their "civil" records.

The widespread distribution of the *Rebellion Records* enhances the value of the works. Over 11,000 copies were originally printed. They were available to essentially anyone who cared to use them. However, accessibility had become a problem prior to the Civil War Centennial as original copies had been destroyed by time, wear and poor storage. Modern reprint editions and microform versions allow researchers local access to the compilations. The collections of major regional, metropolitan and university libraries include both the Army and Navy compilations. (Appendix VI enumerates the various reprints of the *Rebellion Records.*)

CHAPTER VIII

LIMITATIONS

Despite the unquestioned value of the *Official Records*, researchers must recognize their limitations. For all their usefulness, no study should rely on them exclusively. The very fact that the *Rebellion Records* were not edited for accuracy, is, not only an important asset, but also a significant liability. The researcher must balance the data from the *Rebellion Records* with material from other reference books or manuscripts to confirm facts, figures, dates, spellings and other details. Other than errors inherent in reproducing reports without editing the documents, researchers need to be mindful of unintentional errors or oversights made by the compilers. In addition, the *O.R.* can be criticized for "obscuring much of the war's social reality," notably the role of blacks as both soldiers and workers.[1]

Dates attributed to minor battles and local operations are often inaccurate. A master chronology for the *Official Records, Armies* was developed from several sources, including contemporary newspaper accounts. Errors in dates published in these sources were not always corrected by the *OR-Armies* editors. The most blatant inaccuracy in dating is the listing of a skirmish in Spencer, West Virginia on June 16, 1862 when it actually occurred two years later.[2] This certainly must be attributable to a copying or typographical error.

An additional limitation of the *Official Records, Armies* is that about one-third of the operations in the Civil War are not documented in the work. In particular, reports about, or even mention of, a large number of skirmishes, especially in Arkansas and Louisiana are not found in the *OR-Armies* but can be found in contemporary regional newspapers.[3] In defense of the *OR-Armies*, those operations that were omitted were generally fairly minor or of local interest. However, the researcher needs to be aware of those omissions.

Scholars also need to recognize that, in many cases, the Union and Confederate names for the same engagement were different. Though there were no hard and fast rules, typically Confederate officers named battles after the nearest town while their Union counterparts frequently used the name of the nearest stream or body of water. Though, in some cases, the individual book indexes of the *OR-Armies* will lead the user to Union and Confederate reports and papers by looking up only one of names, often both terms must be known to locate all pertinent material.

The researcher also needs to be aware that casualty statistics listed in the *OR-Armies* may be misleading. Too often casualties are listed by brigade rather than by smaller units. This can be misrepresentative in cases where an individual regiment or battery bore the brunt of the fighting. The percentage of losses for the brigade as a whole might be quite low, whereas, when calculated for an individual regiment or battery, could be devastatingly high.

It should be recognized, too, that to say the *Rebellion Records* were not edited for accuracy should not be construed as meaning that no changes were made in the documents. The *OR-Armies* editors did some inconsistent editing. Due to space considerations, only excerpts of reports were often selected for publication. In some cases, when taken out of their full context, explanatory material may be omitted with the result that reports and correspondence may take on a different shade of meaning.

Although editorial policy allowed no change in facts or content, correction of grammar and rewording for readability apparently was allowed. For example, in an original manuscript, a superior officer commended three junior officers for "their coolness and bravery, displayed while under a severe fire from the enemy, and for their prompt execution of orders and their general soldier-like conduct in the field of battle. They done their part well." The version appearing in the *OR-Armies* indicates the three were commended "for their gallant conduct when exposed to the combined fires of the enemy's muskets and artillery, their prompt obedience of all orders. They have performed their part well."[4] While not altering the basic substance of the original report, the edited text has subtle differences in meaning and feeling.

When practical, the researcher may wish to examine the original manuscript to see if it will reveal any significant omission or rewrite. The original manuscripts, or copies thereof, are available in the National Archives.

The user must also recognize that the *Rebellion Records* (or any historical document, for that matter) are reports and correspondence written by men with their attendant human foibles, fears and egos. Some officers, like Union Major General George Brinton McClellan and Confederate General Pierre Gustave Toutant Beauregard, peppered their reports with personal opinions. It is, of course, human nature to justify one's actions and cover up inadequacies. Commanding officers were naturally reluctant to admit shortcomings, either in their leadership or in the conduct of their men. It is often difficult to discern from an official report who actually won a battle or skirmish. Defeated officers often attempted to cover up their own mistakes by claiming they had made a "strategic withdrawal" or by shifting blame or responsibility for failure to other officers or units. On the other hand, successful officers often claimed for themselves too much credit for a victory. It is left to the historian to seek possible motives for concealment or misrepresentation of the truth and to ferret out the actual facts in the matter.

Researchers need to be aware of the particular limitations of the Confederate material found in the two compilations. The editors, sensitive to the need to present a balanced representation of Union and Confederate documents, made commendable efforts to solicit and collect elusive Southern material. Confederate material for several significant operations, however, simply was not available to the compilers of the *OR-Armies.* The papers of General Robert E. Lee's Appomattox Headquarters are not to be found in the *OR-Armies.* Confederate reports and correspondence relating to the Seven Days' Battle, Jackson's Valley Campaign, Vicksburg, Gettysburg and the winter of 1864-65 are among the most significant campaigns where Confederate material is lacking in the *OR-Armies* and, to a large extent, anywhere.[5]

Moreover, though much time and effort was spent authenticating documents, there is evidence that some Confederate material may be suspect. In one particular instance, a Confederate document was significantly rewritten for content before it was submitted to the editors of the *OR-Armies.* Professor Richard M. McMurry scrutinized the original diary of Confederate Lieutenant Thomas Bennett Mackall and discovered entries were deleted, added and changed in an apparent attempt to enhance General Joseph E. Johnston's reputation while undermining that of Lieutenant General John Bell Hood.[6] Fortunately, such blatant doctoring of documents seems, however, to have been the exception. Most researchers who have compared original Confederate documents with those published in the *OR-Armies* have found no significant differences in content. Once again, it must be stressed that the researcher should always evaluate material in the *Rebellion Records* carefully, and compare it with other sources to judge whether the data is consistent with other information.

New York Volunteer Infantry Regiment during the Peninsular Campaign at Deveraux Station near Yorktown, Virginia, 1862. Series I of the *OR-Armies* contains thousands of reports of infantry unit actions.

Poe Civil War Collection, Special Collections Division, U.S. Military Academy Library

CHAPTER IX

CONCLUSIONS

Work on the *OR-Armies* and *OR-Navies* spanned 63 years. The fact that the Federal Government continued to support and fund the *Rebellion Records* projects for so many years is, in itself, amazing. It can only be attributed to Congress' recognition of the significance and public demand for publication of the Civil War *Official Records.* As Secretary of War, Elihu Root, wrote in his 1901 annual report referring to *OR-Armies*, ". . . its value, not merely to survivors of the great conflict, but to future generations, will more than justify the cost."[1] Actually the published information in the *OR-Armies* and *OR-Navies* probably saved the Department of Defense (earlier the War Department) more than its entire cost by reducing inquiries which would have required untold staff research and correspondence time.

The greatest tribute to the *Rebellion Records* is the fact that more than 125 years after the end of the Civil War, historians continue to use and value the *Official Records, Armies* and *Official Records, Navies.* ". . . scholars now acknowledge the series as an essential corpus of the most important printed documents of that critical conflict."[2] Their durability as the dominant source of information of the American Civil War cannot be overestimated.

Endnotes

INTRODUCTION

1. National Historical Society, "Announces a Limited Edition Reprinting of the *Official Records . . .*" (Gettysburg, PA: 1971), p. 1.
2. James I. Robertson, Jr. "The War In Words," *Civil War Times Illustrated*, 11 (April, 1972), p. 48.
3. *U.S. Army War College Guide to the Battle of Gettysburg*, ed. by Jay Luvaas and Harold W. Nelson (Carlisle, PA: South Mountain Press, 1986), p. xiii.

CHAPTER I

1. Stetson Conn, *Historical Work In the United States Army, 1862-1954* (Washington, D.C.: U.S. Army Center of Military History, 1980), pp. 1-2.
2. U.S. War Department, *Annual Report, 1901*, vol. 1, part 2 (Washington, D.C.: 1901), p. 1117.
3. Douglas Southall Freeman, *South to Posterity: An Introduction to the Writing of Confederate History*, reprint ed. (Port Washington, NY; Kennikat Press, 1964), pp. 89-90.
4. Harold E. Mahan, "The Arsenal of History: The Official Records of the War of the Rebellion," *Civil War History* 29 (March, 1983), p. 9.
5. *Ibid.*
6. U.S. War Department. *OR-General Index* (Washington, D.C.: 1902), p. xii.
7. (1) *Ibid.*, p. xxi. (2) Mabel E. Deutrich, *Struggle For Supremacy: The Career of General Fred C. Ainsworth* (Washington, D.C.: Public Affairs Press, 1962), p. 62.
8. Charles H. Franklin, comp., *Study On Project of Publication Of "The War of the Rebellion; A Compilation of the Official Records of the Union and Confederate Armies" 1861-1865* (Washington, D.C.: Historical Section, Army War College, 1931), 0479 [microfilm frame].

CHAPTER II

1. Joseph L. Eisendrath, Jr., "Official Records — Sixty-Three Years in the Making," *Civil War History* 1 (March, 1955), p. 89.
2. *OR-General Index*, pp. xvi-xvii.
3. Mahan, "Arsenal of History," p. 11.
4. U.S. War Dept., *Annual Report, 1878*, p. 539.
5. *Ibid.*, 1901, vol. 1, pt. 2, p. 1106.
6. Mahan, "Arsenal of History," pp. 20-21.
7. (1) *Ibid.*, p. 19. (2) U.S. War Dept., *Annual Report, 1901*, p. 1106.
8. "Henry W. Halleck to Edward M. Stanton, May 11, 1865," U.S. War Department, *The War of the Rebellion: A Compilation of the Official Records of the Union and Confederate Armies*, ed. by Captain Robert N. Scott, et al., 70 vols. in 127 parts plus general-index and atlas (Washington, D.C.: U.S. Government Printing Office, 1880-1901), vol. 46, part 3, p. 1132.
9. U.S. Adjutant General. *General Orders*, No. 27 (July 21, 1865).
10. Carl L. Lokke, "The Captured Confederate Records Under Francis Lieber," *American Archivist*, 9 (October, 1946), p. 298.
11. *Ibid.*, p. 310.
12. *Ibid.*, p. 314.
13. "Battle, Reports, Muster Rolls, Returns and Correspondence Wanted," *The Illustrated Confederate War Journal*, 1 (June, 1893), p. 38.
14. "Editorial Paragraphs," *Southern Historical Society Papers*, 6 (December, 1878), p. 292.
15. *Ibid.*, 5 (October, 1878), p. 192.
16. Mahan, "Arsenal of History," p. 16.

CHAPTER II!

1. U.S. War Dept., *Annual Report, 1880*, pp. 573-574.
2. *New York Times*, "A Mammoth Book: Official Records of the Civil War Compiled At Last In 128 Volumes. Cost Nearly Three Millions of Dollars," Magazine Supplement (October 6, 1901), p. 8.
3. Douglas Southall Freeman, *Lee's Dispatches: Unpublished Letters of General Robert E. Lee, C.S.A. to Jefferson Davis and the War Department of the Confederate States of America, 1862-1865*, new ed. (New York: G. P. Putnam's Sons, 1957), p. xiii.

4. U.S. War Dept., *Annual Report, 1901*, p. 1111.
5. Franklin, p. 7.
6. "Sundry Civil Act, March 3, 1903," National Archives, Record Group 94, Entry 720.

CHAPTER IV

1. U.S. War Department, *The Official Atlas of the Civil War*, intr. by Henry Steele Commager. (New York: Thomas Yoseloff, 1958), p. iii.
2. (1) Theodore Lyman. "Uselessness of the Maps Furnished to the Staff of the Army of the Potomac Previous to the Campaign of May 1864," *Papers of the Military Historical Society of Massachusetts*, vol. 4 (Boston: Military Historical Society of Massachusetts, 1905), p. 79. (2) Richard Taylor, *Destruction and Reconstruction: Personal Experiences of the Late War*, ed. by Richard B. Harwell. (New York: Longmans, Green & Co., 1959), p. 99.
3. Richard W. Stephenson, comp. *Civil War Maps*, 2nd ed. (Washington, D.C.: Library of Congress, 1989), p. 6.
4. Albert H. Campbell, "The Last War Maps of the Confederates," *Century Magazine*, 35 (1888), pp. 479-481.
5. (1) *Civil War Maps: A Graphic Index to the Atlas to Accompany the Official Records of the Union and Confederate Armies*, ed. by Noel S. O'Reilly, David C. Bosse and Robert W. Karrow, Jr. Chicago: Newberry Library, 1987), p. 7. (2) Jedediah Hotchkiss, *Make Me a Map of the Valley: The Civil War Journal of Stonewall Jackson's Topographer* (Dallas, TX: Southern Methodist University Press, 1973), p. 309.
6. *Official Atlas of the Civil War*, Commager, p. iii.
7. (1) U.S. War Department, *Secretary of War Annual Report, 1896* (Washington, D.C.: 1896), pp. 622-623 and 629. (2) U.S. War Department. Military Secretary's Office, "Official Records of the Union and Confederate Armies": Regulations Relating to Distribution and Sale," Washington, D.C.: 1904, p. 3.
8. U.S. War Department, *The Official Military Atlas of the Civil War*, intr. by Richard Sommers (New York: Fairfax Press, 1983), p. ii. Original maps, available at the National Archives should be consulted when scale is critical in the historical analysis. Furthermore, researchers should note that the 1983 reprint edition done by Fairfax Press was reduced in size by 10%.

CHAPTER V

1. James G. Walker, "Bureau of Navigation" in *Report of the Secretary of Navy, 1888* (Washington, D.C.: 1888), p. 83.

2. Bess Glenns, "Navy Department Records in the National Archives," *Military Archives*, 7 (Winter, 1943), p. 250.
3. Kenneth W. Munden and Henry Putney Beers, *Guide to Federal Archives Relating to the Civil War* (Washington, D.C.: National Archives, 1962), p. 449.
4. J. W. McElroy, *Office of Naval Records and Library, 1882-1946* (Washington, D.C.: U.S. Navy Department, 1946), p. 6.
5. "Library and Naval War Records," *Annual Reports of the Navy Department for the Year, 1901*, part 1 (Washington, D.C.: U.S. Government Printing Office, 1901), pp. 121-122. The naval agent appointed by Congress to collect naval documents is not identified in either archival or printed sources.
6. Patricia L. Faust, ed., *Historical Times Illustrated Encyclopedia of the Civil War* (New York: Harper & Row, 1986), p. 583.
7. James Morton Callahan, *Diplomatic History of the Southern Confederacy* (New York: Frederick Ungar Publishing Co., 1964), p. 20.
8. Everett Beach Long, "The Official Records: A Primer of Their Usage," *Civil War Book Club Review* 4 (February, 1960), p. 3.
9. "Library and Naval War Records," *Annual Report of the Navy Department, 1905* (Washington, D.C.: U.S. Government Printing Office, 1906), p. 83.

CHAPTER VI

1. Civil War Centennial Commission, *Military Operations of the Civil War: A Guide-Index to the Official Records of the Union and Confederate Armies, 1861-1865* (Washington, D.C.: 1966), p. v.
2. *Ibid.*, p. v.
3. *Ibid.*, p. vi.
4. *Index to Place Names Mentioned in the War of the Rebellion: A Compilation of the Official Records of the Union and Confederate Armies*, ed. by Dennis A. Gibson (Lafayette: University of Southwestern Louisiana, 1975).
5. Dallas Irvine, comp. *Military Operations of the Civil War: A Guide-Index to the Official Records of the Union and Confederate Armies, 1861-1865*, vol. 1 (Washington, D.C.: U.S. Government Printing Office, 1977), pp. 1-2.
6. *Civil War Maps . . .*, comp. by O'Reilly.
7. 60th Congress, 1st Session, House Document No. 434 (Washington, D.C.: 1907), p. 2.
8. (1) Broadfoot Publishing Co., *The Official Records of the Union and Confederate Navies In the War of the Rebellion* [brochure] (Wilmington, N.C.: 1987). (2) United States Navy Department. *OR-Navies, General Index.* Washington, D.C.: 1927.
9. U.S. General Services Administration, "Guide-Index Expanded for Civil War Records in Archives," *News Release*, Nov. 18, 1877, p. 2.

CHAPTER VII

1. Dallas D. Irvine, "The Genesis of the Official Records," *Mississippi Valley Historical Review* (September, 1937), p. 222.

CHAPTER VIII

1. Mahan, p. 26.
2. Dallas D. Irvine, "A Revelation About the Civil War," unpublished article (Washington, D.C.: Author, 1970), p. 4.
3. Anne Bailey, Ph.D., correspondence with author, Statesboro, GA, August 21, 1989.
4. Richard Dillon, "Which Dispatch Do You Read?" *Manuscripts* 17 (Fall, 1965), pp. 4-5.
5. (1) Freeman, *South to Posterity*, p. 96. (2) *Lee's Dispatches*, pp. vii-xlvi.
6. Richard M. McMurry, "The Mackall Journal and Its Antecedents," *Civil War History* 20 (December, 1974), pp. 311-328.

CHAPTER IX

1. U.S. War Department. *Annual Report of the U.S. War Department*, vol. 1, part 1 (Washington, D.C.: U.S. Government Printing Office, 1901), p. 28.
2. William S. Dudley, "World War I and Federal Military History," *Public Historian*, 12 (Fall, 1990), p. 24.

Bibliography

Aimone, Alan Conrad. "Official Data Gold Mine: The Official Records of the Civil War," *Lincoln Herald*, LXXIV (Winter, 1972), 192-202.

Ambrose, Stephen E. *Halleck: Lincoln's Chief of Staff* (Baton Rouge: Louisiana State University Press, 1962).

"The Assistant Secretary of the Navy," *Harper's Weekly* (vol. 34, no. 1755, August 9, 1890), 627.

Callahan, James Morton. "The Confederate Diplomatic Archives — The Pickett Papers," *South Atlantic Quarterly*, 2 (January, 1903), 1-9.

____________. *The Diplomatic History of the Southern Confederacy.* NY: F. Ungar, 1964.

Campbell, Albert. "The Lost War Maps of the Confederates," *Century Magazine*, 35 (no. 3, 1888), 479-81.

Canan, H. V. "Maps for the Civil War," *Armor*, 65 (Sept.-Oct., 1956), 34-42.

Carnahan, J. Worth. *Civil War Battles from Official Records*, 1899 reprint ed. Fort Davis, TX: Frontier Book Co., 1971.

"Civil War Maps," *American Archivist*, vol. 15, 1952, 267.

Civil War Maps: A Graphic Index to the Atlas to Accompany the Official Records of the Union and Confederate Armies, ed. by Noel S. O'Reilly, David C. Bosse and Robert W. Karrow, Jr., Occasional Publication No. 1. Chicago: The Newberry Library, 1987.

Conn, Stetson. *Historical Work In the United States Army, 1862-1954.* Washington, D.C.: U.S. Army Center of Military History, 1980.

Deutrich, Mabel E. "Fred C. Ainsworth: The Story of A Vermont Archivist," Vermont Historical Society, vol. 27, January, 1959, 22-33.

____________. *Struggle for Supremacy: The Career of General Fred C. Ainsworth.* Washington, D.C.: Public Affairs Press, 1962.

Dillon, Richard. "Which Dispatch Do You Read?" *Manuscripts*, 17 (no. 4, Fall, 1965), 3-5.

Eisendrath, Jr. Joseph L. "The Official Records, Sixty-Three Years In the Making," *Civil War History*, 1 (March, 1955), 89-94.

Floyd, Dale E. *The Southeast During the Civil War; Selected War Department Records in the National Archives of the United States*, Reference Information Paper No. 69. Washington, D.C.: National Archives and Record Service, 1973.

Franklin, Charles H. *Study On the Project of Publication of "The War of the Rebellion: A Compilation of the Official Records of the Union and Confederate Armies, 1861-1865,"* comp. by the Historical Section, Army War College. Washington, D.C.: 1931.

Freeman, Douglas Southall. "An Address: Douglas Southall Freeman," *Civil War History* (March, 1955), 7-15.

____________. *Calendar of Confederate Papers.* NY: Kraus Reprint Co., 1969.

____________. *The South to Posterity: An Introduction to the Writing of Confederate History.* Port Washington, NY: Kennikat Press, 1964.

Freidel, Frank. *Francis Lieber: Nineteenth-Century Liberal.* Baton Rouge: Louisiana State University Press, 1947.

Glenn, Bess. "Navy Department Records In the National Archives," *Military Affairs*, 7 (Winter, 1943), 247-252.

Hart, Albert Bushnell. "The Historical Opportunity In America," *American Historical Review*, 4 (no. 1, October, 1898), 8.

Hotchkiss, Jedediah. *Make Me a Map Of the Valley: The Civil Journal of Stonewall Jackson's Topographer*, ed. by Archie P. McDonald. Dallas, TX: Southern Methodist University Press, 1973.

The Illustrated Confederate War Journal. New York: War Journal Publishing Company, 1893.

Index to Louisiana Place Names Mentioned in the War of the Rebellion, ed. by Dennis A. Gibson. Lafayette: University of Southwestern Louisiana, 1975.

Irvine, Dallas D. "Archives Office of the War Department — Depository of Captured Confederate Archives, 1866-1881," *Military Affairs,* 10 (Spring, 1946), 93-111.

___________. "Fate of Confederate Archives," *American Historical Review,* 44 (July, 1939), 823-841.

___________. "Genesis of the Official Records," *Mississippi Valley Historical Review* (September, 1937), 221-229.

___________. "A Revelation About the Civil War," unpublished article Washington, D.C.: Author, 1970, 1-6.

___________. "Rootstock of Error," *Prologue: The Journal of the National Archives.* (Spring, 1970), 10-14.

J. B. F. "Official Records of the War of the Rebellion," *Journal of the Military Service Institution of the U.S.* (no. 10, 1882), 288.

Kerr, Robert Washington. *History of the Government Printing Office, (At Washington, D.C.) With a Brief Record of the Public Printing For A Century, 1789-1881*, 1881 reprint. New York: Burt Franklin, 1970.

Lilley, David A. "Anticipating the Atlas to Accompany the Official Records: Post-War Mapping of Civil War Battlefields," *Lincoln Herald* (no. 84, Spring, 1982), 37-42.

___________. "Antietam Battlefield Board and Its Atlas: Or the Genesis of the Corman-Cope Maps," *Lincoln Herald* (no. 82, Summer, 1980), 380-387.

Lokke, Carl L. "The Captured Confederate Records Under Francis Lieber," *American Archivist,* 9 (October, 1946), 277-319.

Long, Everett Beach. "The Official Records — Bulwark of Civil War Research," *Civil War Book Club Review* (vol. 4, no. 10, July, 1952), 2-3.

__________. "The Official Records, A Primer of Their Usage," *Civil War Book Club Review* (vol. 4, no. 12, February, 1960), 2-3.

Lyman, Theodore. "Uselessness of the Maps Furnished to Staff of the Potomac Previous to the Campaign of May 1864," *Papers of the Military Historical Society of Massachusetts: The Wilderness Campaign, May-June 1864*, vol. 4 (Boston: Military Historical Society of Massachusetts, 1905), 79-80.

McElroy, J. W. *Office of Naval Records and Library, 1882-1946.* Washington, D.C.: Navy Department, 1946.

McMurry, Richard M. "The Atlanta Campaign of 1864: A New Look," *Civil War History* (vol. 22, March, 1976), 5-15.

__________. "The Mackall Journal and Its Antecedents," *Civil War History* (vol. 20, no. 4, December, 1974), 311-328.

Mahan, Harold E. "Arsenal of History: The Official Records of the Rebellion," *Civil War History* (vol. 29, March, 1983), 5-27.

"A Mammoth Book: *Official Records of the Civil War* Compiled At Last in 128 Volumes. Cost Nearly Three Millions of Dollars," review of the *OR* in the *New York Times Magazine Supplement* (October 6, 1901), 8.

"More About Printing," *Confederate Veteran* (April, 1903), 151.

Morgan, William James and Joye L. Leonhart. *History of the Dudley Knox Center for Naval History.* Washington, D.C.: Dudley Knox Center for Naval History, 1981.

Muntz, A. Philip. "Union Mapping In the American Civil War," *Imago Mundi* (vol. 17, 1963), 90-94.

Naisawald, Louis V. "New Look In Military History: A Comparison of the United States Army's Historical Treatment of the American Civil War and World War," *Military Review* (September, 1954), 13-18.

National Archives. Record Group 94, entry 720, "Sundry Civil Act, March 3, 1903."

Nettsheim, D. D. "Topographic Intelligence and the American Civil War," masters thesis. Fort Leavenworth, KS: U.S. Army Command and General Staff College, 1978.

Nichols, James L. "Confederate Map Supply," *Military Review* (vol. 46; January-February, 1954), 28-32.

"Official Records of the War of the Rebellion — Comment," *Military Historian & Economist* (vol. 1, April, 1916), 199-200.

"Our War Documents," *Military Historian and Economist*, 3 (January, 1918), 1-6.

Pease, Theodore Calvin. "A Caution Regarding Military Documents," *American Historical Review* (vol. 26, October, 1920-July, 1921), 282-283.

Purifay, John. "The Memory Not Trustworthy," *Confederate Veteran* (September, 1920), 327.

Reardon, Carol. *Soldiers and Scholars: The U.S. Army and the Uses of Military History, 1865-1920.* Lawrence: University Press of Kansas, 1990.

Rhoads, James B. "Civil War Maps and Mapping," *Military Engineer.* (January, 1957), 38-43.

Riepma, Siert F. "A Soldier-Archivist and His Records," *American Archivist* (vol. 4, July, 1941), 178-187.

Robertson, James Irvin, Jr., "The War In Words," *Civil War Times Illustrated.* (vol. 10, April, 1972), p. 48.

Ross, Joseph B., comp. *Tabular Analysis of the Records of the U.S. Colored Troops and Their Predecessor Units in the National Archives of the United States.* Washington, D.C.: National Archives and Records Service, 1973.

Sauerlender, Philip H. "A Matter of Record: Photography In the *Atlas to Accompany the Official Records of the Union and Confederate Armies*," *History of Photography* (vol. 7, April-June, 1983), pp. 121-124.

U.S. Congress. 55th. 2d Session. House of Representatives. *To Furnish Rebellion Records to Members of the 55th Congress.* Washington, D.C.: Document Number 1536, 1898.

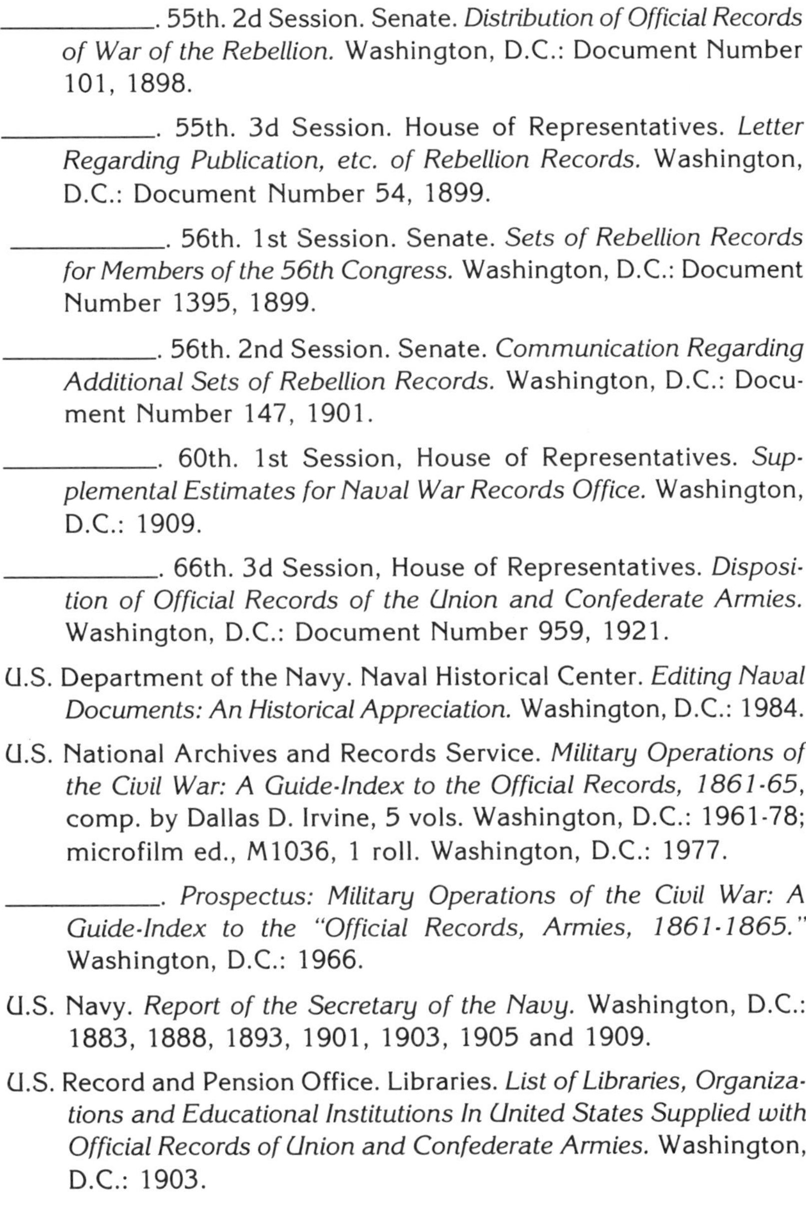

___________. 55th. 2d Session. Senate. *Distribution of Official Records of War of the Rebellion.* Washington, D.C.: Document Number 101, 1898.

___________. 55th. 3d Session. House of Representatives. *Letter Regarding Publication, etc. of Rebellion Records.* Washington, D.C.: Document Number 54, 1899.

___________. 56th. 1st Session. Senate. *Sets of Rebellion Records for Members of the 56th Congress.* Washington, D.C.: Document Number 1395, 1899.

___________. 56th. 2nd Session. Senate. *Communication Regarding Additional Sets of Rebellion Records.* Washington, D.C.: Document Number 147, 1901.

___________. 60th. 1st Session, House of Representatives. *Supplemental Estimates for Naval War Records Office.* Washington, D.C.: 1909.

___________. 66th. 3d Session, House of Representatives. *Disposition of Official Records of the Union and Confederate Armies.* Washington, D.C.: Document Number 959, 1921.

U.S. Department of the Navy. Naval Historical Center. *Editing Naval Documents: An Historical Appreciation.* Washington, D.C.: 1984.

U.S. National Archives and Records Service. *Military Operations of the Civil War: A Guide-Index to the Official Records, 1861-65*, comp. by Dallas D. Irvine, 5 vols. Washington, D.C.: 1961-78; microfilm ed., M1036, 1 roll. Washington, D.C.: 1977.

___________. *Prospectus: Military Operations of the Civil War: A Guide-Index to the "Official Records, Armies, 1861-1865."* Washington, D.C.: 1966.

U.S. Navy. *Report of the Secretary of the Navy.* Washington, D.C.: 1883, 1888, 1893, 1901, 1903, 1905 and 1909.

U.S. Record and Pension Office. Libraries. *List of Libraries, Organizations and Educational Institutions In United States Supplied with Official Records of Union and Confederate Armies.* Washington, D.C.: 1903.

U.S. War Department *Confederate Victories in the Southwest: Prelude to Defeat from the Official Records,* ed. by the publishers. Albuquerque, NM: Horn & Wallace, 1961.

U.S. War Department. *Report of the Chief of Engineers in: Report of the Secretary of War, 1864*, vol. 2. Washington, D.C.: 1865.

____________. *Report of the Secretary of War.* Washington, D.C.: 1874, 1876, 1877, 1878, 1879, 1880, 1884, 1886, 1889, 1892, 1893, 1895, 1896, 1897, 1899, 1900, 1901, 1903 and 1917.

____________. *Union Army Operations In the Southwest: Final Victory from the Official Records*, ed. by the publishers. Albuquerque, NM: Horn & Wallace, 1961.

U.S. War Department. Adjutant General's Office. ". . . Tribute to the memory of Lieutenant Colonel Robert N. Scott," *Army and Navy Journal* (March 12, 1887), 661.

____________. Military Secretary. "Official Records of the Union and Confederate Armies: Regulations Relating to Distribution and Sale," May 12, 1904.

Appendix I

Annotated List Of Selected Reference Sources

A. BIBLIOGRAPHIES

Beers, Henry Putney, comp. *The Confederacy: A Guide to the Archives of the Government of the Confederate States of America.* Washington, D.C.: U.S. Government Printing Office, 1968; reprint, 1986.

This guide explains Confederate archival material within the organization of the National Archives holdings. Reference is also made to pertinent material found in other libraries and archives.

Cole, Garold L. *Civil War Eyewitnesses: An Annotated Bibliography of Books and Articles, 1955-1986* Columbia: University of South Carolina Press, 1988.

Nearly 1,400 published diaries, journals, letters and memoirs written by soldiers, civilians and foreign travelers are described. This work continues the earlier bibliography by Coulter and is particularly useful for fresh insights into how the war was viewed by contemporaries.

Coulter, E. Merton. *Travels in the Confederate States* (Norman: University of Oklahoma Press, 1961).

An excellent descriptive bibliography of 492 personal recollections by both Northern and Southern military and civilian travelers.

Dornbusch, Charles E. *Military Bibliography of the Civil War*, 4 vols. NY: New York Public Library vols. 1-3 reprint and vol. 4. Dayton, OH: Morningside Press, 1961-87.

Nearly every book and article written about Union and Confederate military units are identified as are biographies of leaders during the war. The bibliography's greatest asset, though, is listings for hard to find material not found in Library of Congress catalogs. Many of these formerly "little known" titles (there are a surprisingly large number of them) are of great historical value. Material in these works supplement information found in the *OR-Armies*. National Union Catalog symbols refer researchers to libraries where these elusive books can be found. The major shortcoming of this bibliography is its lack of any critical evaluations of the material cited.

The Dornbusch bibliography has been used as the basis for two different microfiche Civil War collections now in process. Regimental and company rosters, prisoner of war accounts, maps, promotion and court-martial information, casualty statistics, burial records and biographical sketches will be included as they relate to unit histories. *Regimental Histories of the American Civil War*, published by University Microfilms Inc., is projected to reproduce about 3,500 titles published before 1915. *Civil War Unit Histories* published by University Publications of America is publishing some 2,000 unit and personal narratives cited by Dornbush published from 1861 to 1920. Although most of the titles were cited by Dornbush, numerous additional works are being included as well.

Higham, Robin, ed. *A Guide to the Sources of United States Military History*. Hamden, CT: Archon Books, 1975; Supplement 1, ed. by ______ and Donald J. Mrozek, 1981; Supplement 2, 1986.

This series of guides consists of essays evaluating recent literature, topics requiring further study, primary source material as well as a list of articles, books and dissertations. Of particular interest to Civil War researchers are the "Civil War," "Navy" and "Technology" sections.

Kinnell, Susan K., ed. *Military History of the United States: An Annotated Bibliography.* Santa Barbara, CA: ABD-CLIO, 1986.

This includes an impressive compilation of annotated Civil War articles published before 1985.

Munden, Kenneth W. and Henry Putney Beers, comp. *The Union: A Guide to Federal Archives Relating to the Civil War.* Washington, D.C.: National Archives, 1962; reprint, 1986.

This work is the sequel to Beer's *The Confederacy: A Guide to the Archives of the Government of the Confederate States of America.*

Murdock, Eugene C., ed. *The Civil War In the North: A Selective Annotated Bibliography* (NY: Garland Publishing, 1987).

A useful annotated listing of both books and articles describing Union Civil War military, social and political histories.

Nevins, Allan, James I. Robertson, Jr. and Bell I. Wiley, eds. *Civil War Books: A Critical Bibliography*, 2 vols. Baton Rouge: Louisiana State University Press, 1967-1969; reprint, Wilmington, NC: Broadfoot Publishing Co., 1984.

Short critiques by historians are provided for 5,700 books and pamphlets published prior to 1969 and listed in the Library of Congress card catalog. Titles are divided into fifteen subject headings with a different expert evaluating works in each section.

Parrish, T. Michael and Robert M. Willingham, Jr. *Confederate Imprints: A Bibliography of Southern Publications from Secessions to Surrender: Expanding and Revising the Earlier Works of Marjorie Crandall and Richard Hardwell.* Austin, TX: Jenkins Publishing Co. and Katonah, NY: Gary A. Foster, 1987.

This is the most complete bibliography of Confederate books, pamphlets, broadsides, maps, pictorial prints and sheet music produced throughout the South during the war yet compiled. The library where each of the 7,984 sources cited can be found is identified.

Smith, Myron J., Jr. *American Civil War Navies: A Bibliography.* American Naval Bibliography, vol. III. Metuchen, N.J.: Scarecrow Press, 1972.

The most complete bibliography of Civil War naval material yet compiled. This volume includes books, articles and government documents.

Southern Historical Association. *Journal of Southern History.* Houston, TX: Rice University, quarterly, 1935 to date.

The annual "Southern History in Periodical . . .: A Selected Bibliography," features entries under "Military and Naval" and "Politics and Government" arranged chronologically.

U.S. Superintendent of Documents. *Checklist of United States Public Documents, 1789-1909,* 3rd ed. rev. and enl., vol. 1 Washington, D.C.: U.S. Government Printing Office, 1911; reprint, NY: Kraus Reprint Corporation, 1962.

This reference book is a detailed listing of all U.S. government documents published before 1909. Civil War era reports and investigations, proceedings, debates, and other official papers by the many and varied government departments and agencies can be identified using this "checklist."

U.S. National Archives and Records Administration. *Military Service Records: A Select Catalog of National Archives Microfilm Publications.* Washington, D.C.: 1985.

The most significant Civil War National Archives record groups have been microfilmed and are available for purchase. This catalog indexes the Civil War "Military Service Records."

Wright, John H., comp. *Compendium of the Confederacy: An Annotated Bibliography, Books — Pamphlets — Serials,* 2 vols. Wilmington, NC: Broadfoot Publishing Co., 1989.

Many Confederate articles from both predominate and minor serials through 1988 not previously indexed in other reference books are found by topic headings. Civilian, fictional, naval and political titles are included with military monographs.

B. BIBLIOGRAPHICAL SOURCES

Callahan, Edward W., ed. *List of Officers of the Navy of the United States and of the Marine Corps from 1775-1900.* NY: L. R. Hamersly & Co., 1901; reprint, Gaithersburg, MD: Olde Soldier Books, Inc., 1989.

This is the best, most complete source for Marine and Navy officers' service records.

Crute, Joseph H. *Confederate Staff Officers, 1861-1865.* Powhatan, VA: Derwent Books, 1982.

This revision of Marcus Joseph Wright's *List of Staff Officers of the Confederate States Army, 1861-1865* identifies the staff members of each Confederate general. This information often helps the researcher locate pertinent reports and correspondence in the *OR-Armies* and other sources.

Groene, Bertram Hawthorne, *Tracing Your Civil War Ancestor.* Winston-Salem, NC. John F. Blair, rev. ed. 1981.

Written for the non-historian, this book provides useful search strategies and suggests sources that may prove useful to the professional historian as well as the family geneologist.

Heitman, Francis B. *Historical Register and Dictionary of the United States Army, from Its Organization, September 29, 1789, to March 2, 1903*, 2 vols. Washington, D.C.: U.S. Government Printing Office, 1903 rev. ed.; reprint, Urbana: University of Illinois Press, 1965.

The register was compiled from original documents of various government departments. The register is useful for determining service records for each U.S. Army officer, including the units served with, military operations engaged in and honors received. In addition, general information about the U.S. Army during the Civil War era is provided.

Hunt, Roger D. and Jack R. Brown. *Brevet Brigadier Generals In Blue.* Gaithersburg, MD: Olde Soldier Books, Inc., 1990.

Biographical sketches of 1,400 Union brevetted brigadier generals are found in this volume. Information includes their civilian careers, burial sites and a portrait of each.

Krick, Robert K. *Lee's Colonels: A Biographical Register of the Field Officers of the Army of Northern Virginia*, 3rd ed., rev. Dayton, OH: Press of Morningside Bookshop, 1991.

This work expands on Marcus J. Wright's *List of Field Officers, Regiments, and Battalions in the Confederate States Army, 1861-1865* and includes information about 1,954 field grade officers who served in Lee's army.

Sellers, John R., comp. *Civil War Manuscripts: A Guide to Collections in the Manuscript Division of the Library of Congress.* Washington, D.C.: Library of Congress, 1986.

This is a guide to the nation's largest single Civil War manuscript depository of over 10,000 separate collections.

U.S. Adjutant General's Office. *Official Army Register of the Volunteer Force of the U.S. Army for the Years 1861-1865*, 8 vols. Washington, D.C.: 1865-67; reprint, Gaithersburg, MD: Olde Soldier Books, Inc., 1987.

This is the best single source for identifying military service records of company and field grade officers.

U.S. Library of Congress. *National Union Catalog of Manuscript Collections*, 27 vols. Washington, D.C.: 1959 to date, annual.

An annotated survey of the larger United States and Canadian manuscript collections which have been reported to the Library of Congress.

U.S. Naval War Records Office. *Register of Officers of the Confederate States Navy, 1861-1865*, rev. ed. Washington, D.C.: U.S. Government Printing Office, 1931; reprint, Mattituck, NY: J. M. Carroll & Co., 1983.

Revised and expanded from the 1898 edition, this register identifies Confederate naval officers.

Warner, Ezra J. *General In Blue: Lives of the Union Commanders.* Baton Rouge: Louisiana State University Press, 1964; reprint, 1981.

____________. *Generals In Gray: Lives of the Confederate Commanders.* Baton Rouge: Louisiana State University Press, 1959; reprint, 1981.

Generals in Gray contains biographical sketches, statistics and photographs of 425 Confederate generals while *Generals in Blue* includes similar information on 583 Union officers. The appendix enumerates which Union generals opposed which Confederate generals in each battle as well as statistics.

C. CHRONOLOGIES

Long, Everett Beach. *Civil War Day By Day: An Almanac, 1861-1865*, Garden City, NY: Doubleday, 1971; reprint, NY: Da Capa Paperback, 1985.

This work provides a concise account of all noteworthy events each day of the war. The "Special Studies" sections contains the most accurate Civil War statistics to be found. The ninety page bibliography is an excellent reference in itself; it lists those articles, books and manuscripts the author considered to be most reliable. Originally published in 1971, the bibliography was not updated in the reprint.

Moore, Frank, ed. *Rebellion Record: A Diary of American Events, With Documents, Narratives, Illustrative Incidents, Poetry*, 12 vols. NY: 1861-68; reprint, Gettysburg, PA: Civil War Times Illustrated, 1979.

Although some information contained in these volumes is not accurate, this compilation provides an excellent source for newspaper reports, eyewitness accounts and anecdotal material about the war. The *Official Records* compilers used this work to determine chronology so errors in dates in this work are often repeated in the *OR-Armies.*

U.S. Naval History Division. *Civil War Naval Chronology, 1861-65*, 6 parts. Washington, D.C.: U.S. Government Printing Office, 1961-66; reprint, 1975.

This work provides a day-by-day detailed chronology of naval events as well as yearly summaries.

Warinner, N. E., comp. *A Register of Military Events In Virginia.* Richmond: Virginia Civil War Commission, 1959.

A reliable source for studying the military events in Virginia throughout the Civil War.

D. DICTIONARIES

Boatner, Mark Mayo, III. *Civil War Dictionary*, rev. ed. NY: David McKay Co., 1988.

This volume is particularly valuable for brief campaign and battle summaries. Other military related entries, for example "firearms," are informative and useful, as well. Entries describing "civil affairs" are generally not as well done as are military subjects.

Encyclopedia of Southern History, ed. by David C. Roller and Robert W. Twyman (Baton Rouge: Louisiana State University Press, 1979).

Comprehensive coverage of significant people, events, movements, institutions and issues related to southern history is provided in this book. Though not exclusively dedicated to Civil War topics, well over half the information is directly or indirectly related to the War of the Rebellion.

Faust, Patricia L., ed. *Historical Times Illustrated Encyclopedia of the Civil War.* (NY: Harper & Row, 1986).

This work, done by a team of historians, covers fewer topics than Boatner's *Civil War Dictionary*, however, entries tend to be better researched and more detailed.

E. EDITED PUBLISHED PAPERS OF LEADING CIVIL WAR FIGURES

Modern collected papers identify and clarify — with footnotes — people, places and events referred to in the original documents. With editors' hindsight, facts are verified and subjects are placed in historical perspective. "Letter press editions" which print manuscript letters and documents in an easy to read format, are typically arranged chronologically. In general, introductions summarize events covered in that volume.

It is often expedient to use these collected papers to learn about events and people associated with a prominent person because the editors identify people, places and events. Typically, the collected works are well-indexed with complete listings of people, places and events mentioned in each volume.

Civil War Papers of George B. McClellan, Selected Correspondence, 1860-1865, ed. by Stephen W. Sears. New York: Ticknor & Fields, 1989.

Official records collected by Major General McClellan from 1861 to 1862 were not available to the editors of the *OR-Armies*. The Sears edited correspondence includes many of these missing official papers.

Collected Works of Abraham Lincoln, ed. by Roy P. Basler, 8 vols. New Brunswick, NJ: Rutgers University Press, 1953-55; supplement, 1832-1865, vol. 9. Westport, CT: Greenwood Press, 1974; supplement, 1832-1865, vol. 10. New Brunswick: 1990 and Roy P. Basler and Christian Basler, ed. supplement, 1848-1865, vol. 11. New Brunswick: 1990.

Lee's Dispatches: Unpublished Letters of General Robert E. Lee, C.S.A. to Jefferson Davis and the War Department of the Confederate States of America, 1862-1865, ed. by Douglas Southall Freeman, new ed. NY: G. P. Putnam's Sons, 1957.

Papers of Andrew Johnson, ed. by LeRoy P. Graf, 9 vols. published to date. Knoxville: University of Tennessee Press, 1967 to date.

Papers of Jefferson Davis, ed. by Lynda Lasswell Crist and Mary Seaton Dix, 9 vols. published to date. Baton Rouge: Louisiana State University Press, 1971 to date.

Papers of Ulysses Simpson Grant, ed. by John Y. Simon, 18 vols. published to date. Carbondalle: Southern Illinois University Press, 1967 to date.

Wartime Papers of R. E. Lee, ed. by Clifford Dowdey. Boston: Virginia Civil War Commission, 1961.

F. ILLUSTRATED SOURCES

Davis, Keith F. *George W. Barnard: Photographer of Sherman's Campaign*. Kansas City, MO: Hallmark Cards, Inc., 1990.

A study of less known Western Civil War campaign photographs.

Davis, William C. *Image of War, 1861-1865: Shadows of the Storm; Guns of Sixty-Two; Embattled Confederacy: 1861-1865; Fighting for Time; South Besieged and End of an Era*, 6 vol. NY: Doubleday, 1981-1984; reprint, Harrisburg, PA: The National Historical Society, 1991. Supplemented in his *Torched By Fire: A Photographic Portrait of the Civil War*, 2 vols. Boston: Little, Brown and Co., 1985.

The over 4,000 photographs selected by Davis, arranged by subject, are accompanied by well-researched, descriptive narratives. Though many are different images of the same subject or views reproduced in Francis T. Miller's *Photographic History of the Civil War*, there is enough variation to warrant use of both. Davis had access to Civil War photographic collections not available seventy years earlier when Miller's work was compiled.

Frassanito, William A. *Antietam: The Photographic Legacy of America's Bloodiest Day*. New York: Charles Scribner's Sons, 1978; *Gettysburg: A Journey in Time*. New York: Scribner's, 1974; and *Grant and Lee: The Virginia Campaigns, 1864-1865*. New York: Scribner's, 1983.

In this outstanding trilogy, the compiler, an expert Civil War photographic historian, analyzes each of three major campaigns through the use of contemporary photographs.

Miller, Francis Trevelyan and Robert S. Lanier, ed. *Photographic History of the Civil War*, 10 vols. NY: Reviews of Reviews Co., 1911; reprint, 12 vols. bound in 6 books, Secacus, NJ: Blue & Grey Press, 1987.

This landmark photographic source includes the largest published collection of Matthew Brady photographs, along with those of other notable photographers. Compiled shortly after the completion of the *Official Records*, thousands of photographs are arranged by subject and accompanied by descriptive text. Although some photographs were inaccurately identified, this continues to be a significant and valuable photographic source.

Time-Life Books. *The Civil War*, 28 vols. Alexandria, VA: 1987.

The popular series covers various topics with text, contemporary photographs, paintings and modern colored photographs of artifacts.

Todd, Frederick Porter. *American Military Equipage, 1851-1872*, 3 vols. Providence, RI and NY: Scribner, Company of Military Historians, 1975-1983.

The most detailed descriptive and illustrated survey of the subject. The American Civil War soldier's, sailor's and marine's uniforms and equipment are emphasized.

G. MEMOIR SOURCES

Confederate Veteran. Nashville, TN: 1893-1932; reprint, 40 vols. plus 3 vols. index. Wilmington, NC: Broadfoot Publishing Co., 1990.

This set of magazines contains one of the largest collections of Confederate memoirs, anecdotes, incidents and personal stories; more Confederate enlisted soldier recollections were published in this magazine than in any other single source. The magazine is also notable for its photographs of veterans. It published over one thousand post war photographs of veterans, as well as reunion pictures and "memorial" photographs of deceased veterans. The recently completed three volume index cites subjects and names of officers, soldiers and units.

Johnson, Robert Underwood and Clarence Clough Buel, ed. *Battles and Leaders of the Civil War*, 4 vols. bound in 8 books. NY: Century Magazine, 1887-1888; latest reprint, Hicksville, NY: Archive Society, 1991.

This classic series of 300 articles illustrated by 1,700 drawings, woodcuts, etchings and photographs was written by some

250 high ranking Union and Confederate officers. The articles are organized by theaters of operation, campaigns and battles. The set continues to be a standard reference for information on battles and campaigns, despite the biases and distortions in some of the articles.

Military Historical Society of Massachusetts, *Papers of the Military Historical Society of Massachusetts*, 15 vols. Boston: 1896-1918; reprint, Wilmington, NC: Broadfoot Publishing Co., 1990.

This series of papers was originally read before the Military Historical Society of Massachusetts by field grade officers. Papers on all the theaters of the war, as well as the naval subjects, are included. Some of the accounts are opinionated and cover controversial subjects. The series of unofficial accounts and observations supplements the *Official Records.*

Military Order of the Loyal Legion of the United States, 1883-1909. Various serial publications by state commanderies.

These provide insights about conditions, scenes, attitudes, impressions and observations not found in the *Official Records.* The recollections of enlisted soldiers and officers often provide significantly different views of the same actions and personalities.

Southern Historical Society. *Southern Historical Papers*, 52 vols. Richmond, VA: 1876-1959; reprint with a 2 vol. index, Wilmington, NC: Broadfoot Publishing Co., 1990-91.

No other single source except the *Official Records* contains more material on life in the fighting forces of the Confederacy. These papers often provide information about battles, skirmishes, activities, etc. not found in the *Official Records.* A number of Confederate reports, particularly the Gettysburg reports and correspondence, were published in the papers but not in the *Official Records.*

H. MILITARY UNIT SOURCES

Crute, Joseph H., Jr. *Units of the Confederate States Army* Midlothian, VA: Derwent Books, 1987.

This work expands upon Marcus Joseph Wright's earlier *List of Field Officers, Regiments, and Battalions in the Confederate States Army, 1861-1865.* Organizations, campaigns, losses and commanders are identified. This can provide a useful guide for further research.

Dyer, Frederick Henry. *A Compendium of the War of the Rebellion, Compiled and Arranged from Official Records of the Federal and Confederate Armies, Reports of the Adjutant Generals of the Several States*, 3 vols. Des Moines, IA: Dyer Publishing Co., 1908; reprint, 1 vol., Dayton, OH; Morningside Bookshop, 1990.

This work is the most useful source for information related to Union military units. The 900 pages provide a brief resume of over 2,000 Federal military units. No one has yet attempted a similar concise source for Confederate military units.

Fox, William F. *Regimental Losses In the American Civil War, 1861-1865.* Albany, NY: Albany Publishing Co., 1989; reprint, Dayton, OH: Morningside Bookshop, 1985.

One of the most cited general references, this volume is the classic source for Union casualty statistics of the "Three Hundred Fighting Regiments."

Tancig, William Jere, comp. *Confederate Military Land Units, 1861-1865.* NY: Thomas Yoseloff, 1967.

The compilation identifies all Confederate regiments, battalions, companies and batteries by their official designations as well as by their "nicknames." This work is essentially a revision of the Confederate section of William Frayne Amann's *Personnel of the Civil War.*

U.S. Department of the Navy. Naval Historical Center. *Dictionary of American Naval Fighting Ships*, 8 vols. Washington, D.C.: 1959-1981.

The source provides histories of all U.S. Naval vessels with illustrations and statistics. Approximately one third of the ships cited saw service during the Civil War.

U.S. Quartermaster's Department. *Commanders of Army, Corps, Divisions and Brigades, U.S. Army, 1861-1865.* Philadelphia: Burke & McFetridge, 1888.

This organizational chart follows the succession of Union field commanders — officers in charge of armies, corps, divisions and brigades — throughout the war. Commanders' full names, titles and dates of command are listed. Knowing the availability of this chart, published in 1888, the editors of the *OR-Armies* elected not to include this information.

Welcher, Frank J. *The Union Army, 1861-1865: Organization and Operations*, 2 vols. Bloomington: Indiana University Press, 1989- .

Welcher describes the formation, composition and organizational evolution of Union military units above the regimental level. It is an expansion of Dyer's *Compendium, of the War of the Rebellion.* Volume I traces the movement of Union armies and corps through the Eastern theater battles and campaigns while volume II provides that same information for the Western Theater. Although most of the information in these volumes can be found in the *OR-Armies*, this work provides a more concise source to trace major Union army movements.

APPENDIX II

Union Department & Commission Reports Relating To The Civil War

*Unless noted otherwise, all publications were published by the U.S. Government Printing Office.

Barnard, John G. *Report of the Defenses of Washington to the Chief of Engineers, U.S. Army*. Washington, D.C.: 1871.

___________. and W. F. Barry. *Report of the Engineer and Artillery Operations from Its Organization of the Army of the Potomac to the Close of the Peninsula Campaign.* NY: Van Nostrand, 1863.

Chickamauga and Chattanooga National Military Park Commission. *Battle of Chickamauga, Georgia, September 19-20, 1863, Organization of the Army of the Cumberland and the Army of the Tennessee*; comp. by H. V. Boynton. Washington, D.C.: 1895.

___________. *Battles About Chattanooga, Tennessee, November 23-25, 1863; Orchard Knob, Lookout Mountain, Missionary Ridge; Organization of Union Forces and Confederate Forces*, comp. by H. V. Boynton. Washington, D.C.: 1895.

___________. *Campaign for Chattanooga, Historical Sketch, Descriptive Model In Relief of Region About Chattanooga and of Battles Illustrated* . . . Washington, D.C.: 1902.

___________. *Campaign for Chattanooga, Theater of Movements and Battlefields As Seen From Point of Lookout Mountain.* Washington, D.C.: 1902.

___________. *Legislation, Congressional and State, Pertaining to Establishment of Park; Regulations, Original and Amended, Governing Erection of Monuments, Markers and Other Memorials.* Washington, D.C.: 1897.

___________. *Progress and Condition of Work of Establishing Chickamauga and Chattanooga National Military Park.* Washington, D.C.: 1895.

___________. *Report of Chickamauga and Chattanooga National Park Commission On Claim of John B. Turchin and Others That In Battle of Chattanooga His Brigade Captured Position Missionary Ridge Known as the De Long Place.* Washington, D.C.: 1896.

Gettysburg National Military Park Commission. *Annual Reports.* Washington, D.C.: 1893- .

Grant, Ulysses Simpson. *Official Report of Lieutenant General Ulysses S. Grant Embracing a History of the Operations of the Armies of the Union, from March, 1862, to the Closing Scenes of the Rebellion.* NY: Beadle and Co., 1865.

___________. *Report of Lieutenant General U. S. Grant of the Armies of the United States, 1864-1865.* Washington, D.C.: 1865.

Hancock, Winfield Scott. *Official Reports of the Military Operations of Major General W. S. Hancock, 1861-1865.* NY: 1882.

Haupt, Herman. *Photographs, Illustrative of Operations In Construction and Transportation as Used to Facilitate the Movement of the Armies of the Rappahannock of Virginia and the Potomac Including Experiments Made to Determine the Most Practical and Expeditious Modes to Be Resorted to In the Construction, Destruction and Reconstruction of Roads and Bridges.* Boston: Wright & Potter Printers, 1863.

McClellan, George B. *Letter of the Secretary of War Transmitting Report on the Organization of the Army of the Potomac, and its Campaigns in Virginia and Maryland, Under Command of George B. McClellan, July 26, 1861-November 7, 1862.* Washington, D.C.: 1864 (38th Congress, 1st Session, House Executive Document 15, serial number 1187); reprinted, NY: Sheldon and Co., 1864.

Otis, George Alexander. *Report On the Extent and Nature of the Materials Available for the Preparation of a Medical and Surgical History of the Rebellion*, Circular No. 6, Surgeon General's Office. Philadelphia: J. B. Lippincott, 1865.

Pope, John. *Letter from the Secretary of War . . . Transmitting Copy of Report of Major John Pope.* 37th Congress, 3d Session, House of Representatives, Document number 81. Washington, D.C.: 1863.

U.S. Adjutant General's Office. *Alphabetical List of Battles of the War of the Rebellion.* Washington, D.C.: 1881.

___________. *Chronological List of Battles, Engagements, etc. During the Rebellion, 1860-65, with the Designation of Troops Engaged,* comp. from the records of the Adjutant General's Office. Washington, D.C.: 1875.

___________. *Comparative Statement of the Number of Men Furnished and the Deaths In the United States Army During the Late War.* Washington, D.C.: 1886.

___________. *Desertion, Removal of Charge of Desertion (Act for Relief of Certain Volunteer and Regular Soldiers of Civil War and War With Mexico and Amendments).* Washington, D.C.: 1902.

___________. *General Orders.* Washington, D.C.: 1861-65, reprinted in bound volumes at the year's end. Other general orders, circulars and memoranda were also issued by the headquarters of the various U.S. Army departments.

___________. *Itinerary of the Army of the Potomac and Co-operating Forces In the Gettysburg Campaign, June 5-July 31, 1864: Organization of the Army of the Potomac and Army of Northern Virginia At the Battle of Gettysburg; and Return of Casualties In the Union and Confederate Forces*, comp. by Richard C. Drum, 3rd ed. Washington, D.C.: 1888.

___________. *List of Battles, Engagements, Skirmishes, etc., During the Rebellion of 1861, with Dates and Designation of Troops Engaged.* Washington, D.C.: 1873.

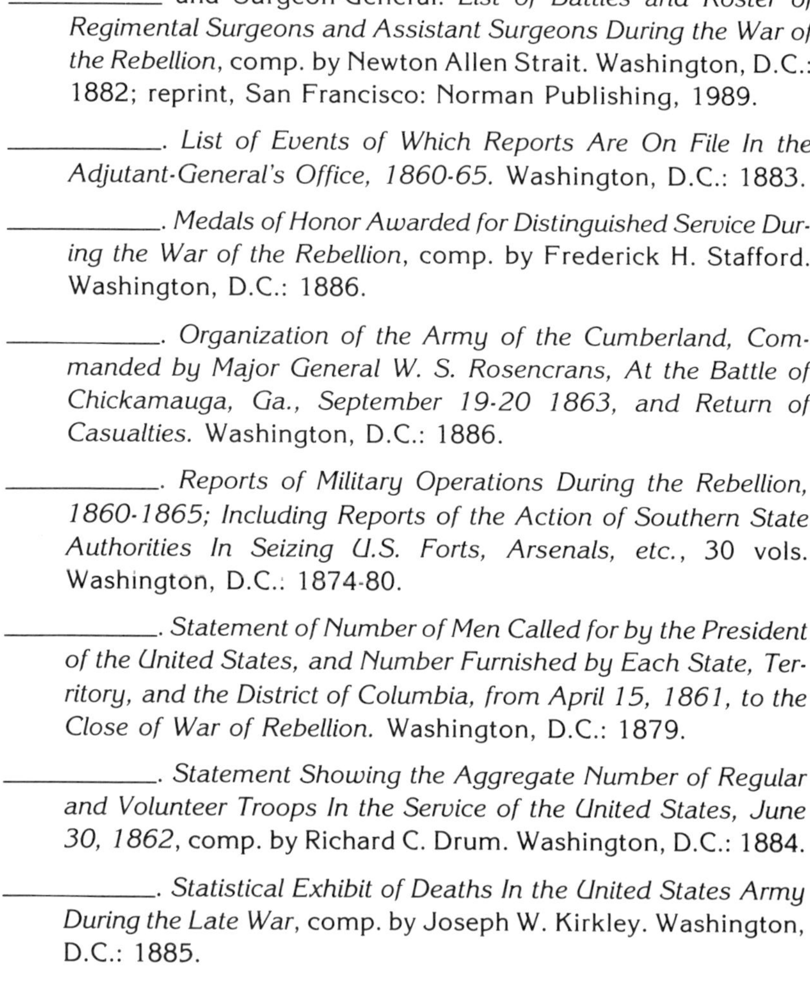

——— and Surgeon-General. *List of Battles and Roster of Regimental Surgeons and Assistant Surgeons During the War of the Rebellion*, comp. by Newton Allen Strait. Washington, D.C.: 1882; reprint, San Francisco: Norman Publishing, 1989.

———. *List of Events of Which Reports Are On File In the Adjutant-General's Office, 1860-65.* Washington, D.C.: 1883.

———. *Medals of Honor Awarded for Distinguished Service During the War of the Rebellion*, comp. by Frederick H. Stafford. Washington, D.C.: 1886.

———. *Organization of the Army of the Cumberland, Commanded by Major General W. S. Rosencrans, At the Battle of Chickamauga, Ga., September 19-20 1863, and Return of Casualties.* Washington, D.C.: 1886.

———. *Reports of Military Operations During the Rebellion, 1860-1865; Including Reports of the Action of Southern State Authorities In Seizing U.S. Forts, Arsenals, etc.*, 30 vols. Washington, D.C.: 1874-80.

———. *Statement of Number of Men Called for by the President of the United States, and Number Furnished by Each State, Territory, and the District of Columbia, from April 15, 1861, to the Close of War of Rebellion.* Washington, D.C.: 1879.

———. *Statement Showing the Aggregate Number of Regular and Volunteer Troops In the Service of the United States, June 30, 1862*, comp. by Richard C. Drum. Washington, D.C.: 1884.

———. *Statistical Exhibit of Deaths In the United States Army During the Late War*, comp. by Joseph W. Kirkley. Washington, D.C.: 1885.

U.S. Army. Corps of Engineers. *Permanent Fortifications and Sea-Coast Defenses.* Report Number 86, 37th Congress, 2nd Session, House of Representatives. Washington, D.C.: 1862.

U.S. Army Engineer School. *Professional Memoirs, U.S. Corps of Engineers*, vols. 2-8 and 11. Washington, D.C.: 1910.

U.S. Coast and Geodetic Survey. *Military and Naval Service of the United States Coast Survey, 1861-1865.* Washington, D.C.: 1916.

U.S. Congress. *Congressional Globe*, 23rd Congress to 42nd Congress, 2 December 1833-3 March 1873, 46 vols. in 109 books. Washington, D.C.: *The Globe*, 1834-1873.

____________. *Report of the Joint Committee On the Conduct of the War.* 37th Congress, 3rd Session. Washington, D.C.: 1863; House of Representatives, Executive Documents; reprint, Millwood, NY: Kraus Reprint Co., 1977.

Part 1 — Army of the Potomac
Part 2 — Bull Run and Ball's Bluff
Part 3 — Department of the West

38th Congress, 2nd Session. Washington, D.C.: 1865.

Vol. 1 — Reports on the Army of the Potomac and the Battle of Petersburg
Vol. 2 — Reports on the Red River Expedition, Fort Fisher Expedition and Heavy Ordnance
Vol. 3 — Reports on Sherman-Johnson, Light Draught Monitors, Massacre of Cheyenne Indians, Ice Contracts, Rosecrans' Campaigns & Misc.

38th Congress, 2nd Session, Supplemental Report. Washington, D.C.: 1866.

Part 1 — Reports of Sherman and Thomas
Part 2 — Reports of Pope, Foster, Pleasanton, Hitchcock, Sheridan, Ricketts, Communication & Memorial of Norman Wiard

U.S. Department of State. *Papers Relating to Foreign Affairs, Accompanying the Annual Message of the President*, 19 vols. Washington, D.C.: 1861-1868.

U.S. Military Railroad Department. *United States Military Railroads. Report of Brevet Brigadier General D. C. McCallum, Director and General Manager, from 1861 to 1866.* Washington, D.C.: 1866.

U.S. Military Secretary's Department. *Memorandum Relative to the General Officers In the Armies of the United States During the Civil War - 1861-1865.* Washington, D.C.: 1908. U.S. Naval War Records Office. *Calendar, 1860-1865.* Washington, D.C.: 1904.

____________. *Chronological Tables, December 26, 1860 - November 6, 1865.* Washington, D.C.: 1895.

____________. *List of Log Books of U.S. Naval Vessels, 1861-1865, on File in the Navy Department.* Washington, D.C.: 1898.

____________. *List of U.S. Naval Vessels, 1861-1865; including the Ellet Ram Fleet and Mississippi Marine Brigade. Appendix List of U.S. Coast Survey Vessels, 1861-1865.* Washington, D.C.: 1891.

____________. *List of War Charts.* Washington, D.C.: 1889.

U.S. Navy. *Letter of the Secretary of the Navy . . . Connected with the Recent Engagements on the Mississippi River, Which Resulted in the Capture of Forts Jackson, St. Philip and the City of New Orleans, the Destruction of the Rebel Flotilla, etc.* 37th Congress, 2d Session, Senate Document number 56 Washington, D.C.: 1864.

____________. *Ordinance Instructions for the United States Navy.* Washington, D.C.: 1866.

____________. *Report of the Secretary of the Navy . . . Reports from Officers, December 1863.* Washington, D.C.: 1863.

____________. *Report of the Secretary of the Navy with an Appendix Containing Reports from Officers, December 1864.* Washington, D.C.: 1864.

____________. *Report of the Secretary of the Navy in Relation to Armored Vessels.* Washington, D.C.: 1864.

U.S. Pension Bureau. *List of Pensioners on the Roll, January 1, 1883; Giving the Name of Each Pensioner, the Cause for Which Pensioned, the Post-Office Address, the Rate of Pension Per Month, and the Date of Original Allowance, as Called For by Senate Resolution of December 8, 1882*, 5 vols. Washington, D.C.: 1883.

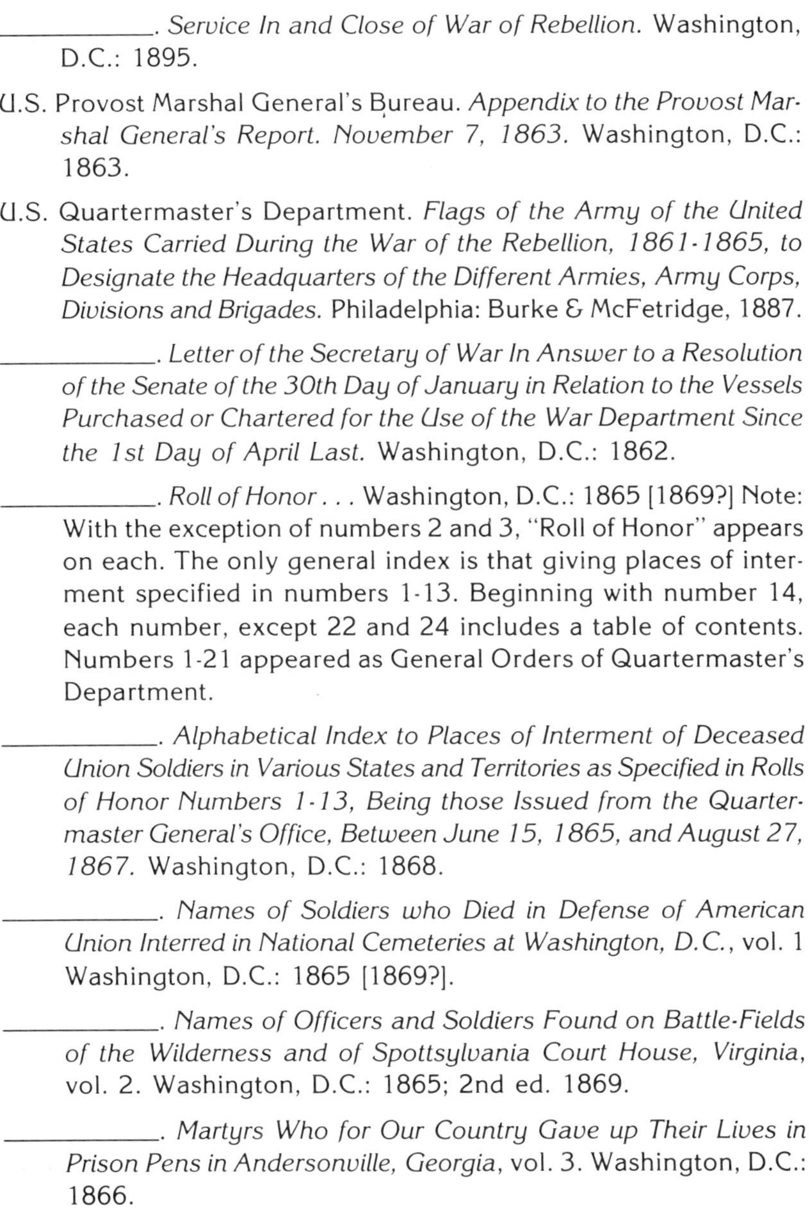

__________. *Service In and Close of War of Rebellion.* Washington, D.C.: 1895.

U.S. Provost Marshal General's Bureau. *Appendix to the Provost Marshal General's Report. November 7, 1863.* Washington, D.C.: 1863.

U.S. Quartermaster's Department. *Flags of the Army of the United States Carried During the War of the Rebellion, 1861-1865, to Designate the Headquarters of the Different Armies, Army Corps, Divisions and Brigades.* Philadelphia: Burke & McFetridge, 1887.

__________. *Letter of the Secretary of War In Answer to a Resolution of the Senate of the 30th Day of January in Relation to the Vessels Purchased or Chartered for the Use of the War Department Since the 1st Day of April Last.* Washington, D.C.: 1862.

__________. *Roll of Honor . . .* Washington, D.C.: 1865 [1869?] Note: With the exception of numbers 2 and 3, "Roll of Honor" appears on each. The only general index is that giving places of interment specified in numbers 1-13. Beginning with number 14, each number, except 22 and 24 includes a table of contents. Numbers 1-21 appeared as General Orders of Quartermaster's Department.

__________. *Alphabetical Index to Places of Interment of Deceased Union Soldiers in Various States and Territories as Specified in Rolls of Honor Numbers 1-13, Being those Issued from the Quartermaster General's Office, Between June 15, 1865, and August 27, 1867.* Washington, D.C.: 1868.

__________. *Names of Soldiers who Died in Defense of American Union Interred in National Cemeteries at Washington, D.C.*, vol. 1 Washington, D.C.: 1865 [1869?].

__________. *Names of Officers and Soldiers Found on Battle-Fields of the Wilderness and of Spottsylvania Court House, Virginia*, vol. 2. Washington, D.C.: 1865; 2nd ed. 1869.

__________. *Martyrs Who for Our Country Gave up Their Lives in Prison Pens in Andersonville, Georgia*, vol. 3. Washington, D.C.: 1866.

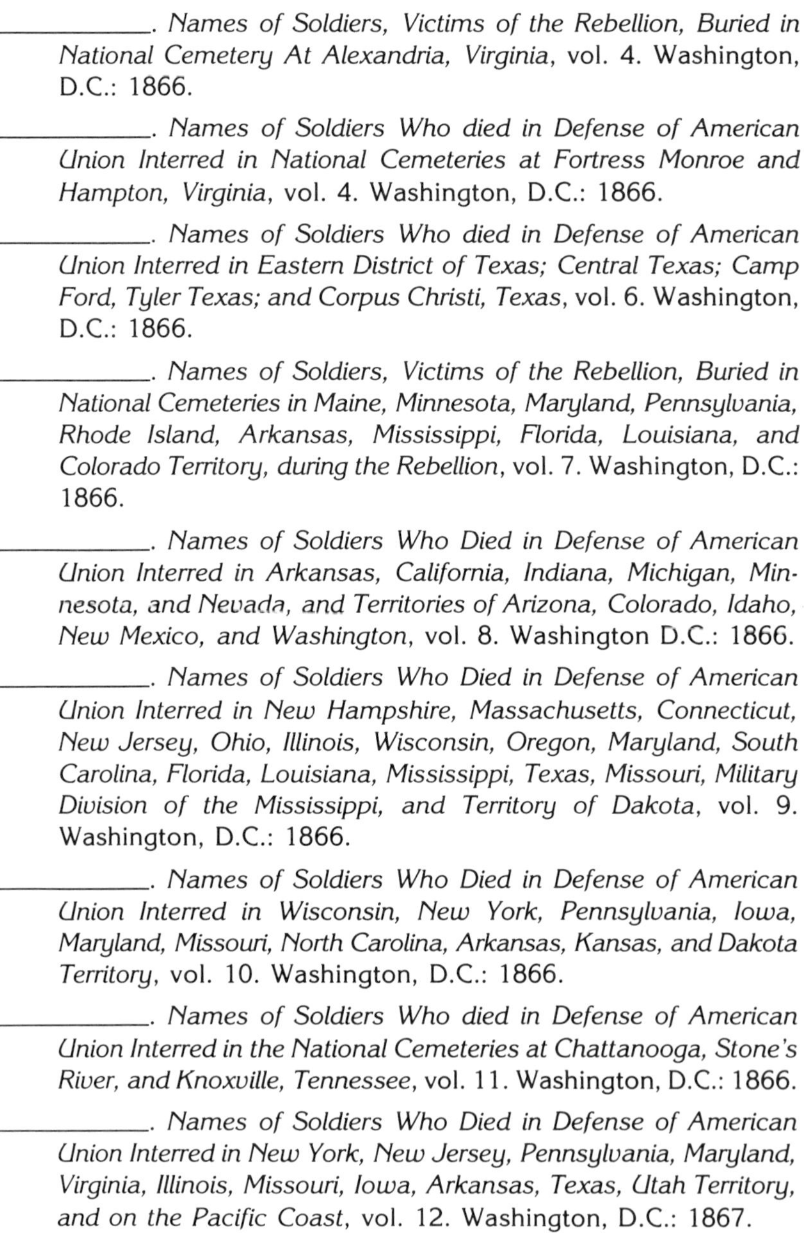

___________. *Names of Soldiers, Victims of the Rebellion, Buried in National Cemetery At Alexandria, Virginia*, vol. 4. Washington, D.C.: 1866.

___________. *Names of Soldiers Who died in Defense of American Union Interred in National Cemeteries at Fortress Monroe and Hampton, Virginia*, vol. 4. Washington, D.C.: 1866.

___________. *Names of Soldiers Who died in Defense of American Union Interred in Eastern District of Texas; Central Texas; Camp Ford, Tyler Texas; and Corpus Christi, Texas*, vol. 6. Washington, D.C.: 1866.

___________. *Names of Soldiers, Victims of the Rebellion, Buried in National Cemeteries in Maine, Minnesota, Maryland, Pennsylvania, Rhode Island, Arkansas, Mississippi, Florida, Louisiana, and Colorado Territory, during the Rebellion*, vol. 7. Washington, D.C.: 1866.

___________. *Names of Soldiers Who Died in Defense of American Union Interred in Arkansas, California, Indiana, Michigan, Minnesota, and Nevada, and Territories of Arizona, Colorado, Idaho, New Mexico, and Washington*, vol. 8. Washington D.C.: 1866.

___________. *Names of Soldiers Who Died in Defense of American Union Interred in New Hampshire, Massachusetts, Connecticut, New Jersey, Ohio, Illinois, Wisconsin, Oregon, Maryland, South Carolina, Florida, Louisiana, Mississippi, Texas, Missouri, Military Division of the Mississippi, and Territory of Dakota*, vol. 9. Washington, D.C.: 1866.

___________. *Names of Soldiers Who Died in Defense of American Union Interred in Wisconsin, New York, Pennsylvania, Iowa, Maryland, Missouri, North Carolina, Arkansas, Kansas, and Dakota Territory*, vol. 10. Washington, D.C.: 1866.

___________. *Names of Soldiers Who died in Defense of American Union Interred in the National Cemeteries at Chattanooga, Stone's River, and Knoxville, Tennessee*, vol. 11. Washington, D.C.: 1866.

___________. *Names of Soldiers Who Died in Defense of American Union Interred in New York, New Jersey, Pennsylvania, Maryland, Virginia, Illinois, Missouri, Iowa, Arkansas, Texas, Utah Territory, and on the Pacific Coast*, vol. 12. Washington, D.C.: 1867.

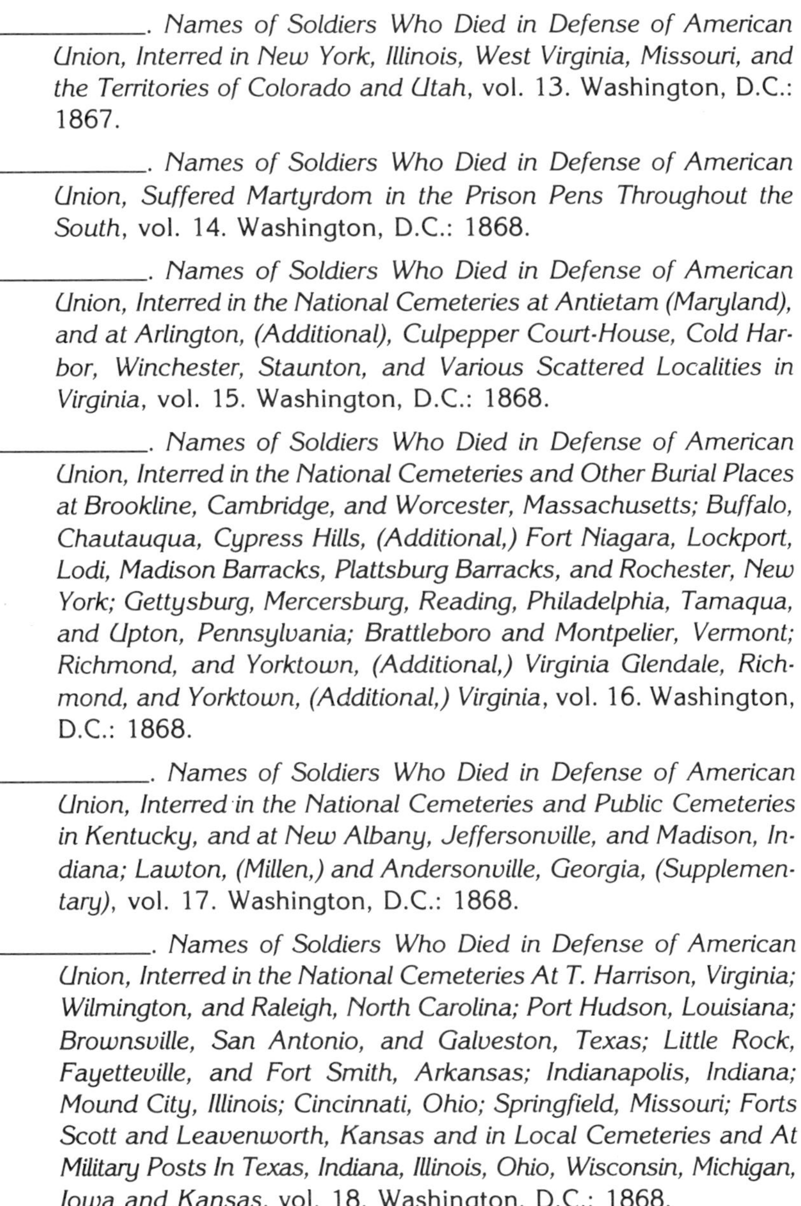

___________. *Names of Soldiers Who Died in Defense of American Union, Interred in New York, Illinois, West Virginia, Missouri, and the Territories of Colorado and Utah*, vol. 13. Washington, D.C.: 1867.

___________. *Names of Soldiers Who Died in Defense of American Union, Suffered Martyrdom in the Prison Pens Throughout the South*, vol. 14. Washington, D.C.: 1868.

___________. *Names of Soldiers Who Died in Defense of American Union, Interred in the National Cemeteries at Antietam (Maryland), and at Arlington, (Additional), Culpepper Court-House, Cold Harbor, Winchester, Staunton, and Various Scattered Localities in Virginia*, vol. 15. Washington, D.C.: 1868.

___________. *Names of Soldiers Who Died in Defense of American Union, Interred in the National Cemeteries and Other Burial Places at Brookline, Cambridge, and Worcester, Massachusetts; Buffalo, Chautauqua, Cypress Hills, (Additional,) Fort Niagara, Lockport, Lodi, Madison Barracks, Plattsburg Barracks, and Rochester, New York; Gettysburg, Mercersburg, Reading, Philadelphia, Tamaqua, and Upton, Pennsylvania; Brattleboro and Montpelier, Vermont; Richmond, and Yorktown, (Additional,) Virginia Glendale, Richmond, and Yorktown, (Additional,) Virginia*, vol. 16. Washington, D.C.: 1868.

___________. *Names of Soldiers Who Died in Defense of American Union, Interred in the National Cemeteries and Public Cemeteries in Kentucky, and at New Albany, Jeffersonville, and Madison, Indiana; Lawton, (Millen,) and Andersonville, Georgia, (Supplementary)*, vol. 17. Washington, D.C.: 1868.

___________. *Names of Soldiers Who Died in Defense of American Union, Interred in the National Cemeteries At T. Harrison, Virginia; Wilmington, and Raleigh, North Carolina; Port Hudson, Louisiana; Brownsville, San Antonio, and Galveston, Texas; Little Rock, Fayetteville, and Fort Smith, Arkansas; Indianapolis, Indiana; Mound City, Illinois; Cincinnati, Ohio; Springfield, Missouri; Forts Scott and Leavenworth, Kansas and in Local Cemeteries and At Military Posts In Texas, Indiana, Illinois, Ohio, Wisconsin, Michigan, Iowa and Kansas*, vol. 18. Washington, D.C.: 1868.

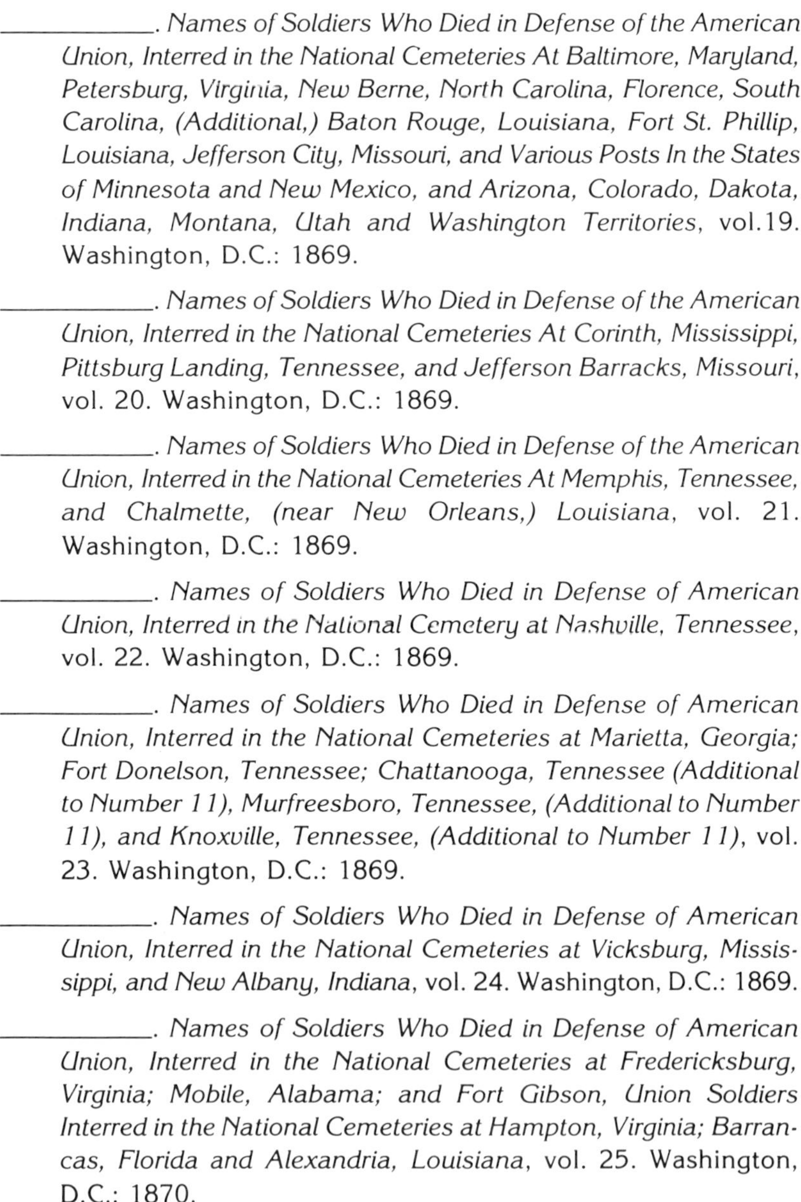

___________. *Names of Soldiers Who Died in Defense of the American Union, Interred in the National Cemeteries At Baltimore, Maryland, Petersburg, Virginia, New Berne, North Carolina, Florence, South Carolina, (Additional,) Baton Rouge, Louisiana, Fort St. Phillip, Louisiana, Jefferson City, Missouri, and Various Posts In the States of Minnesota and New Mexico, and Arizona, Colorado, Dakota, Indiana, Montana, Utah and Washington Territories*, vol.19. Washington, D.C.: 1869.

___________. *Names of Soldiers Who Died in Defense of the American Union, Interred in the National Cemeteries At Corinth, Mississippi, Pittsburg Landing, Tennessee, and Jefferson Barracks, Missouri*, vol. 20. Washington, D.C.: 1869.

___________. *Names of Soldiers Who Died in Defense of the American Union, Interred in the National Cemeteries At Memphis, Tennessee, and Chalmette, (near New Orleans,) Louisiana*, vol. 21. Washington, D.C.: 1869.

___________. *Names of Soldiers Who Died in Defense of American Union, Interred in the National Cemetery at Nashville, Tennessee*, vol. 22. Washington, D.C.: 1869.

___________. *Names of Soldiers Who Died in Defense of American Union, Interred in the National Cemeteries at Marietta, Georgia; Fort Donelson, Tennessee; Chattanooga, Tennessee (Additional to Number 11), Murfreesboro, Tennessee, (Additional to Number 11), and Knoxville, Tennessee, (Additional to Number 11)*, vol. 23. Washington, D.C.: 1869.

___________. *Names of Soldiers Who Died in Defense of American Union, Interred in the National Cemeteries at Vicksburg, Mississippi, and New Albany, Indiana*, vol. 24. Washington, D.C.: 1869.

___________. *Names of Soldiers Who Died in Defense of American Union, Interred in the National Cemeteries at Fredericksburg, Virginia; Mobile, Alabama; and Fort Gibson, Union Soldiers Interred in the National Cemeteries at Hampton, Virginia; Barrancas, Florida and Alexandria, Louisiana*, vol. 25. Washington, D.C.: 1870.

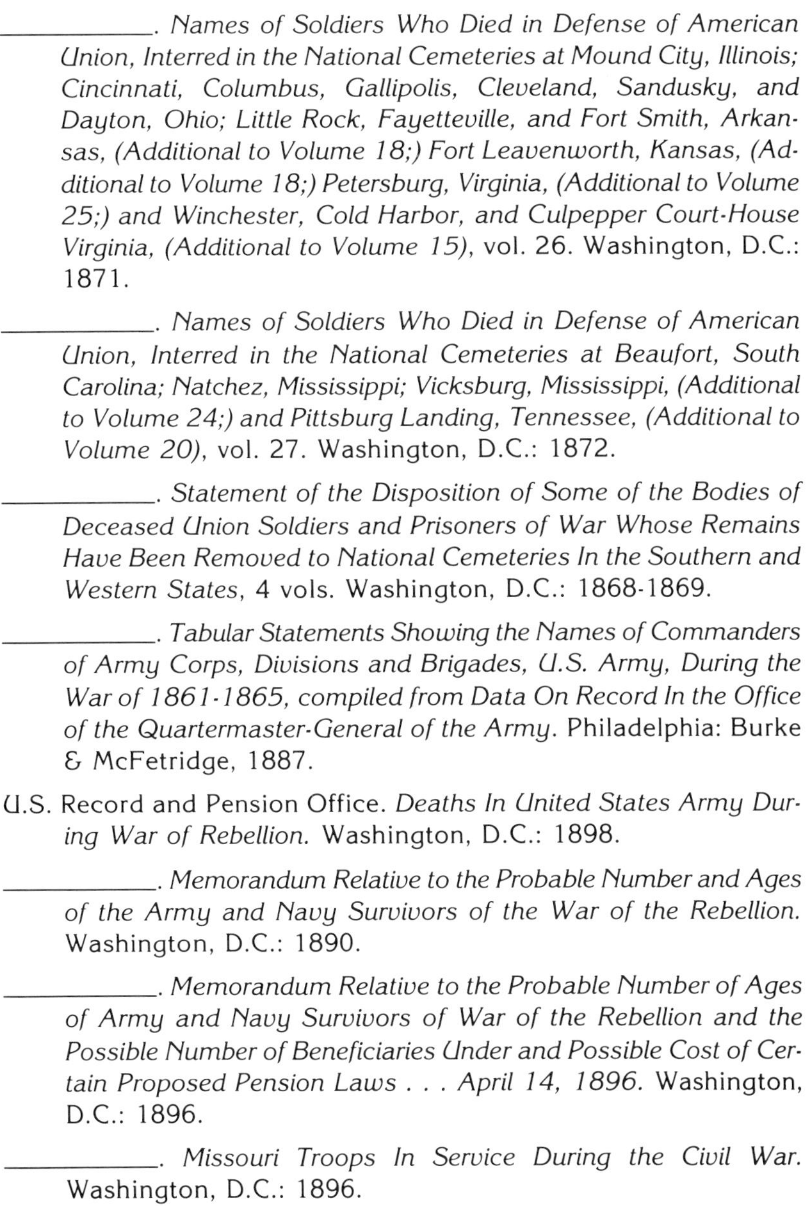

__________. *Names of Soldiers Who Died in Defense of American Union, Interred in the National Cemeteries at Mound City, Illinois; Cincinnati, Columbus, Gallipolis, Cleveland, Sandusky, and Dayton, Ohio; Little Rock, Fayetteville, and Fort Smith, Arkansas, (Additional to Volume 18;) Fort Leavenworth, Kansas, (Additional to Volume 18;) Petersburg, Virginia, (Additional to Volume 25;) and Winchester, Cold Harbor, and Culpepper Court-House Virginia, (Additional to Volume 15)*, vol. 26. Washington, D.C.: 1871.

__________. *Names of Soldiers Who Died in Defense of American Union, Interred in the National Cemeteries at Beaufort, South Carolina; Natchez, Mississippi; Vicksburg, Mississippi, (Additional to Volume 24;) and Pittsburg Landing, Tennessee, (Additional to Volume 20)*, vol. 27. Washington, D.C.: 1872.

__________. *Statement of the Disposition of Some of the Bodies of Deceased Union Soldiers and Prisoners of War Whose Remains Have Been Removed to National Cemeteries In the Southern and Western States*, 4 vols. Washington, D.C.: 1868-1869.

__________. *Tabular Statements Showing the Names of Commanders of Army Corps, Divisions and Brigades, U.S. Army, During the War of 1861-1865, compiled from Data On Record In the Office of the Quartermaster-General of the Army*. Philadelphia: Burke & McFetridge, 1887.

U.S. Record and Pension Office. *Deaths In United States Army During War of Rebellion*. Washington, D.C.: 1898.

__________. *Memorandum Relative to the Probable Number and Ages of the Army and Navy Survivors of the War of the Rebellion*. Washington, D.C.: 1890.

__________. *Memorandum Relative to the Probable Number of Ages of Army and Navy Survivors of War of the Rebellion and the Possible Number of Beneficiaries Under and Possible Cost of Certain Proposed Pension Laws . . . April 14, 1896*. Washington, D.C.: 1896.

__________. *Missouri Troops In Service During the Civil War*. Washington, D.C.: 1896.

____________. Survivors of War of Rebellion. *Memorandum Relative to the Probable Number and Ages of Army and Navy Survivors of War of the Rebellion and Possible Number of Beneficiaries Under and Possible Cost of Proposed Pension Laws.* Washington, D.C.: 1896.

U.S. Senate. Committee on Veterans' Affairs. *Medal of Honor Recipients, 1863-1978.* Washington, D.C.: 1979.

U.S. Signal Office. *Official Reports On Signal Corps Operations, Including Balloons, During Civil War; Reprinted from Official Records of War of Rebellion*, series 3, vol. 3. Washington, D.C.: 1899.

U.S. Subsistence Department. *How to Feed an Army.* Washington, D.C.: 1901.

U.S. Surgeon General's Office. *Chronological Summary of Engagements and Battles.* Washington, D.C.: 1867.

____________. *Medical and Surgical History of the War of the Rebellion, 1861-1865*, 3 vols. in 6 parts. Washington, D.C.: 1870-1888; new ed., *Medical and Surgical History of the Civil War*, 12 vols. Wilmington, NC: Broadfoot Publishing Co., 1990.

____________. *Statistics, Medical and Anthropological, of Provost Marshal General's Bureau, Derived from Records of Examination for Military Service In Armies of United States During the Late War of Rebellion, of Over a Million Recruits, Drafted Men, Substitutes, and Enrolled Men*, comp. by J. H. Baxter, 2 vols. Washington, D.C.: 1875.

U.S. War Department. *Memorandum Relative to the General Officers In the Armies of the United States During the Civil War, 1861-65*, comp. from Official Records. Washington, D.C.: 1906.

____________. Library. *Subject Catalog No. 4: Finding List of Military Biographies and Other Personal Literature In the Library.* Washington, D.C.: 1898; 2nd ed. 1899.

____________. *Subject Catalog No. 5: List of Photographs and Photographic Negatives Relating to the War of the Union Now in the Library.* Washington, D.C.: 1897.

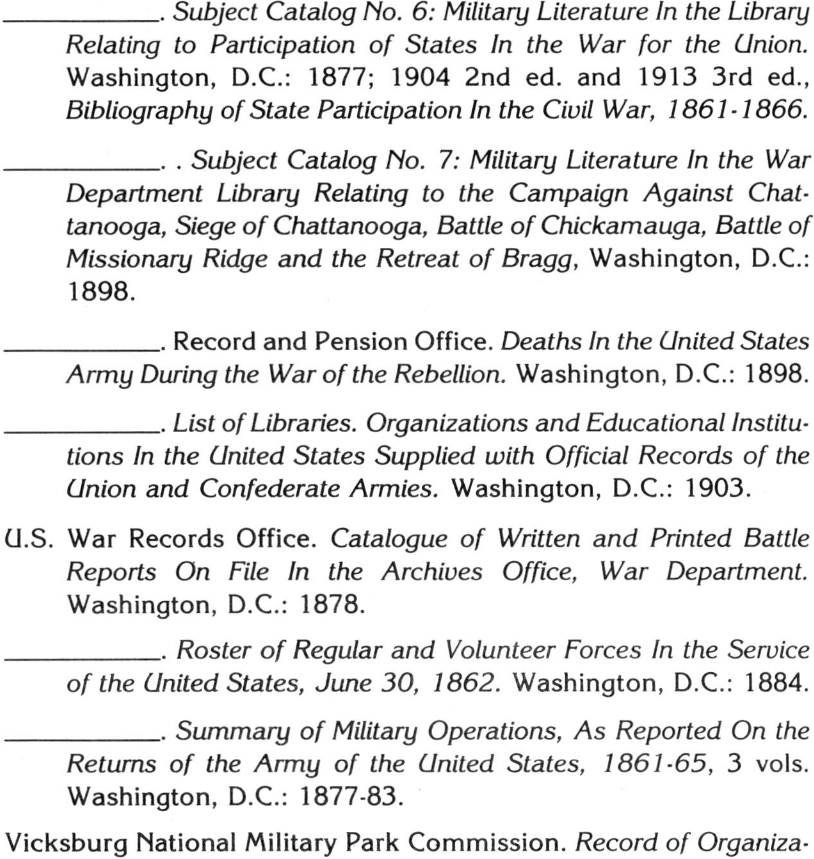

__________. *Subject Catalog No. 6: Military Literature In the Library Relating to Participation of States In the War for the Union.* Washington, D.C.: 1877; 1904 2nd ed. and 1913 3rd ed., *Bibliography of State Participation In the Civil War, 1861-1866.*

__________. . *Subject Catalog No. 7: Military Literature In the War Department Library Relating to the Campaign Against Chattanooga, Siege of Chattanooga, Battle of Chickamauga, Battle of Missionary Ridge and the Retreat of Bragg*, Washington, D.C.: 1898.

__________. Record and Pension Office. *Deaths In the United States Army During the War of the Rebellion.* Washington, D.C.: 1898.

__________. *List of Libraries. Organizations and Educational Institutions In the United States Supplied with Official Records of the Union and Confederate Armies.* Washington, D.C.: 1903.

U.S. War Records Office. *Catalogue of Written and Printed Battle Reports On File In the Archives Office, War Department.* Washington, D.C.: 1878.

__________. *Roster of Regular and Volunteer Forces In the Service of the United States, June 30, 1862.* Washington, D.C.: 1884.

__________. *Summary of Military Operations, As Reported On the Returns of the Army of the United States, 1861-65*, 3 vols. Washington, D.C.: 1877-83.

Vicksburg National Military Park Commission. *Record of Organizations Engaged In Campaign, Siege, and Defense of Vicksburg*, comp. by John S. Kountz. Washington, D.C.: 1901.

Webb, G. W. *List of Engagements Between the Regular Army of the United States and Various Tribes of Hostile Indians Which Occurred during the Years 1790 to 1898, Inclusive.* St. Joseph, MO: 1939.

Wells, John Wesley, comp. *An Alphabetical List of the Battles (with dates) of the War of the Rebellion.* Washington, D.C.: 1875; rev. ed. with N. A. Strait, 1882 and 3rd ed., 1883.

Wooters, William R. *An Alphabetical List of the Battles of the War of the Rebellion with Dates, from Ft. Sumter, S.C., April 12 and 13, 1861, to General Kirby Smith's Surrender, May 26, 1865, comp. from Official Sources.* Philadelphia: W. R. Wooters, 1889.

____________. Record and Pension Office. *Deaths In the United States Army During the War of the Rebellion.* Washington, D.C.: 1898.

____________. *List of Libraries. Organizations and Educational Institutions In the United States Supplied with Official Records of the Union and Confederate Armies.* Washington, D.C.: 1903.

U.S. War Records Office. *Catalogue of Written and Printed Battle Reports On File In the Archives Office, War Department.* Washington, D.C.: 1878.

____________. *Roster of Regular and Volunteer Forces In the Service of the United States, June 30, 1862.* Washington, D.C.: 1884.

____________. *Summary of Military Operations, As Reported On the Returns of the Army of the United States, 1861-65,* 3 vols. Washington, D.C.: 1877-83.

Vicksburg National Military Park Commission. *Record of Organizations Engaged In Campaign, Siege, and Defense of Vicksburg,* comp. by John S. Kountz. Washington, D.C.: 1901.

Webb, G. W. *List of Engagements Between the Regular Army of the United States and Various Tribes of Hostile Indians Which Occurred During the Years 1790 to 1898, Inclusive*; St. Joseph, MO: 1939.

Wells, John Wesley, comp. *An Alphabetical List of the Battles (with dates) of the War of the Rebellion.* Washington, D.C.: 1875; rev. ed. with N. A. Strait, 1882 and 3rd ed., 1883.

Wooters, William R. *An Alphabetical List of the Battles of the War of the Rebellion with Dates, from Ft. Sumter, S.C., April 12 and 13, 1861, to General Kirby Smith's Surrender, May 26, 1865, comp. from Official Sources.* Philadelphia: W. R. Wooters, 1889.

Appendix III

Congressional Documents Relating To The Civil War

These subcommittee reports are found in government depository libraries. Each item can be located according to the Superintendent of Documents serial and document numbers shown in brackets.

Aid Furnished Rebellion by Subjects of Great Britain [1209, 2]

Alabama Claims Commission
- Closing Up of Business of [2359, 567; 2437, 945]
- Distribution of Award by [1708, 243; 2065, 307; 2256, 1032]
- Extension of duration of Court [2253, 190]
- Opinions of, etc., 1876 [1719, 21]

Alabama Claims
- Committee Report on, 1873 [1576, 47]
- Correspondence Concerning Claims Against Great Britain, vol. 1, 1869 [1394, 11], vol. 2 [1395, 11], vol. 3 [1396, 11], vol. 4 [1397, 11] and vol. 5 [1398, 11]
- Diplomatic Correspondence Relative to, 1869 [1405, 10]

Arbitration, Mediation, etc., Looking to Close of War [1149, 38]

Arrests of Citizens by Authority of Secretary of War, and Conditions of Their Discharge [1149, 11]

Articles of War [1105, 84]

Bragg, Braxton, Arrest of, etc. [443, 211]

Bragg, Braxton and Polk, Leonidas, Negotiations with Legal Representatives of, Papers Relative to War of Rebellion, 1880 [1941, 6]

Capture of Vessels of Great Britain Carrying Articles Contraband of War [1149, 27]

Claims Against United States Government
 Allowed Under Act of March 12, 1863, etc., in 1888 [2599, 538]
 Allowed Under Act of July 4, 1864 [1802, 31]

Coffee Extract for Use of Troops [1121, 16]

Committee Reports on Disturbed Condition of Country [1104, 31]

Contracts, Government, Investigation of [1143, 2] same [1144, 2]

Correspondence, James Buchanan to Lewis Cass, Regarding Policy to be Pursued to Avert War [1393, 7]

"Cotton Loan" or Rebel Debt [1263, 95] same [1263, 131]

Debts of Loyal States [1272, 16]

Enrollment Act 1863 [1150, 41]

Exemption Clause [1195, 97]
. . . Reports of Commissioners . . . [1237, 9] same [1255, 22]

Expenses of July 1, 1861-June 30, 1879 [1886, 206]

Honors to Rebels [1267, 141]

Insurrectionary States
 Direct Tax in [1263, 133] same [1708, 46]
 Duties, Collection of, in [1100, 72]
 Judicial Civil Courts in [1237, 19]
 Lands Sold for Taxes in [1407, 98]
 Laws of Late Insurgent States (Rebel Debt) [1262, 131]
 Loyal Citizens in, Claims of [1576, 43] same [1607, 121]
 Money Due [1479, 6]
 Policy of President Toward [1277, 2]
 Taxes in, Collection of, 1863 [1176, 3]
 Trade With, Investigation [1235, 2]

Ironclads, Sales of, Investigation [1358, 64]

Major-Generals Names and Numbers, etc., 1861 [1122, 33]

Mediation, Arbitration, etc., Looking to Close of War [1149, 38]

Message, Commencement of First Session of 37th Congress (specially called) [1112, 1]

Military Services of Citizens of Prussia [1308, 4]

Negotiations with Insurgents [1209, 18]

Ordnance Stores Furnished During Civil War, Payment for [1614, 245]

Pardons by the President of the United States [1289, 31] same [1311, 32] same [1330, 16] same [1339, 179]

Payment of Soldiers, 1863 [1161, 29] same [1161, 37]

Photographic Negatives Illustrative of, Rand-Ordway Collection, Memorial Relating to [2265, 19]

Prisoners, Exchange of [1137, 124] same [1176, 17] same [1223, 20] same [1223, 22] same [1223, 32]
General Grant's Testimony [1211, 119]
Hitchcock's Report, 1865 [1250]
Return, 1864 [1178, 68] same [1202, 67]
State and Political [1209, 23]
Statistics of Deaths, Union and Rebel [1267, 152]
Treatment of, by Rebel Authorities, Testimony, etc., 1869 [1391, 45]

Prize Cases in New York [1194, 74]

Prize Matters [1163, 73]

Prize Money, Distribution of [1187, 25] same [1263, 114]

Prize Vessels [1343, 279]

Rebel Debt or "Cotton Loan" [1263, 95] same [1263, 131]

Reconstruction
Confederate Property in Europe [1345, 304]
Military Prisoners, etc. [1425, 225]

Appendix IV

Confederate Documents And Sources Outside The *Rebellion Records*

A. *OFFICIAL RECORDS* PUBLISHED BY THE CONFEDERATE STATES OF AMERICA

The following Confederate imprints are available either from research libraries or on microfilm from Research Publications, Inc. *Confederate Imprints, 1861-1865*, 99 reels. New Haven, Ct.: 1974.

Confederate States of America. War Department. *Battle of Cedar Run. Report of Lieutenant General Jackson.* (n.p.: 1863).

____________. *Battle of Shiloh: Report of General Polk.* Richmond: 1863?).

____________. *General Beauregard's Official Report of the Battle of Manassas.* (Richmond: 1861).

____________. *General Polk's Report of the Battle of Belmont. Columbus, Ky. November 10, 1861.* (n.p.: 186_).

____________. *Letter from the Secretary of War . . . March 10, 1862.* [transmitting the official report of Col. Wm. B. Tallaferro of the action at Carrock's (i.e., Corrick's) Ford, July 13, 1861] [Richmond: 1862].

____________. *Letter from the Secretary of War . . . March 11th, 1862.* [enclosing the reports of the defence and fall of Fort Donelson.] [Richmond, 1862].

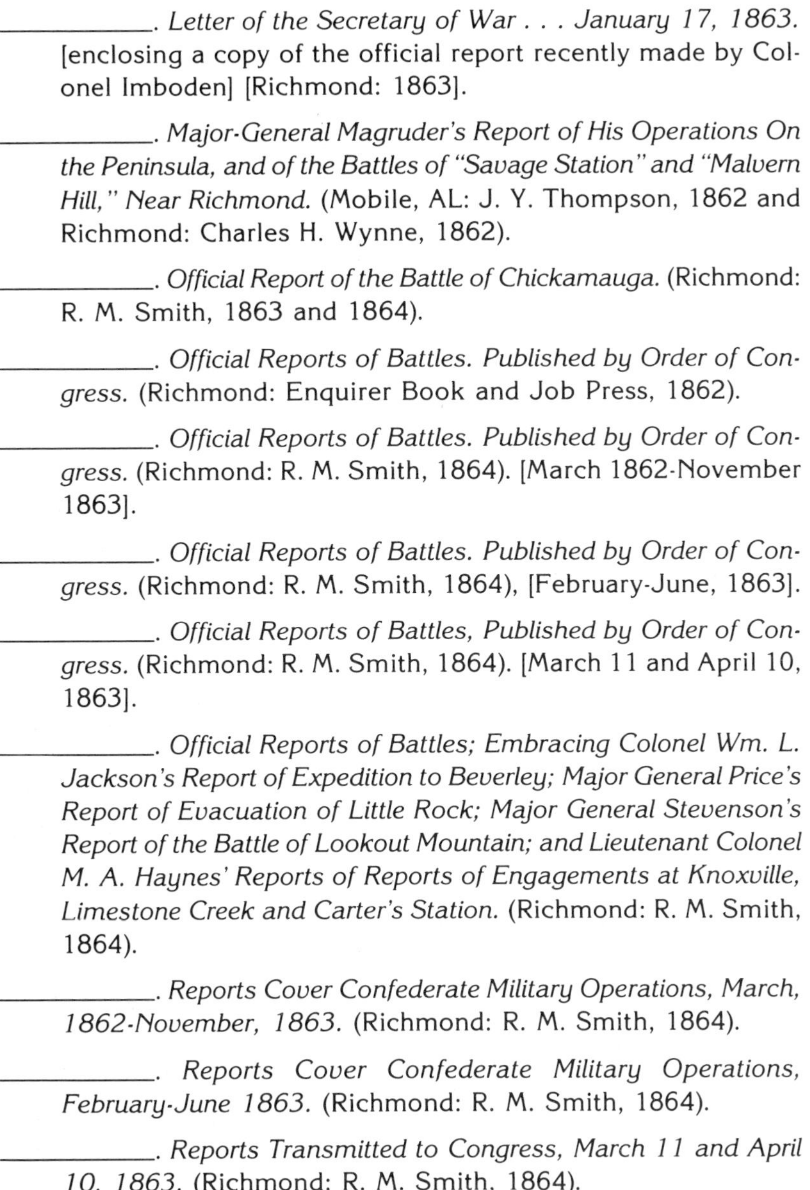

___________. *Letter of the Secretary of War . . . January 17, 1863.* [enclosing a copy of the official report recently made by Colonel Imboden] [Richmond: 1863].

___________. *Major-General Magruder's Report of His Operations On the Peninsula, and of the Battles of "Savage Station" and "Malvern Hill," Near Richmond.* (Mobile, AL: J. Y. Thompson, 1862 and Richmond: Charles H. Wynne, 1862).

___________. *Official Report of the Battle of Chickamauga.* (Richmond: R. M. Smith, 1863 and 1864).

___________. *Official Reports of Battles. Published by Order of Congress.* (Richmond: Enquirer Book and Job Press, 1862).

___________. *Official Reports of Battles. Published by Order of Congress.* (Richmond: R. M. Smith, 1864). [March 1862-November 1863].

___________. *Official Reports of Battles. Published by Order of Congress.* (Richmond: R. M. Smith, 1864), [February-June, 1863].

___________. *Official Reports of Battles, Published by Order of Congress.* (Richmond: R. M. Smith, 1864). [March 11 and April 10, 1863].

___________. *Official Reports of Battles; Embracing Colonel Wm. L. Jackson's Report of Expedition to Beverley; Major General Price's Report of Evacuation of Little Rock; Major General Stevenson's Report of the Battle of Lookout Mountain; and Lieutenant Colonel M. A. Haynes' Reports of Reports of Engagements at Knoxville, Limestone Creek and Carter's Station.* (Richmond: R. M. Smith, 1864).

___________. *Reports Cover Confederate Military Operations, March, 1862-November, 1863.* (Richmond: R. M. Smith, 1864).

___________. *Reports Cover Confederate Military Operations, February-June 1863.* (Richmond: R. M. Smith, 1864).

___________. *Reports Transmitted to Congress, March 11 and April 10, 1863.* (Richmond: R. M. Smith, 1864).

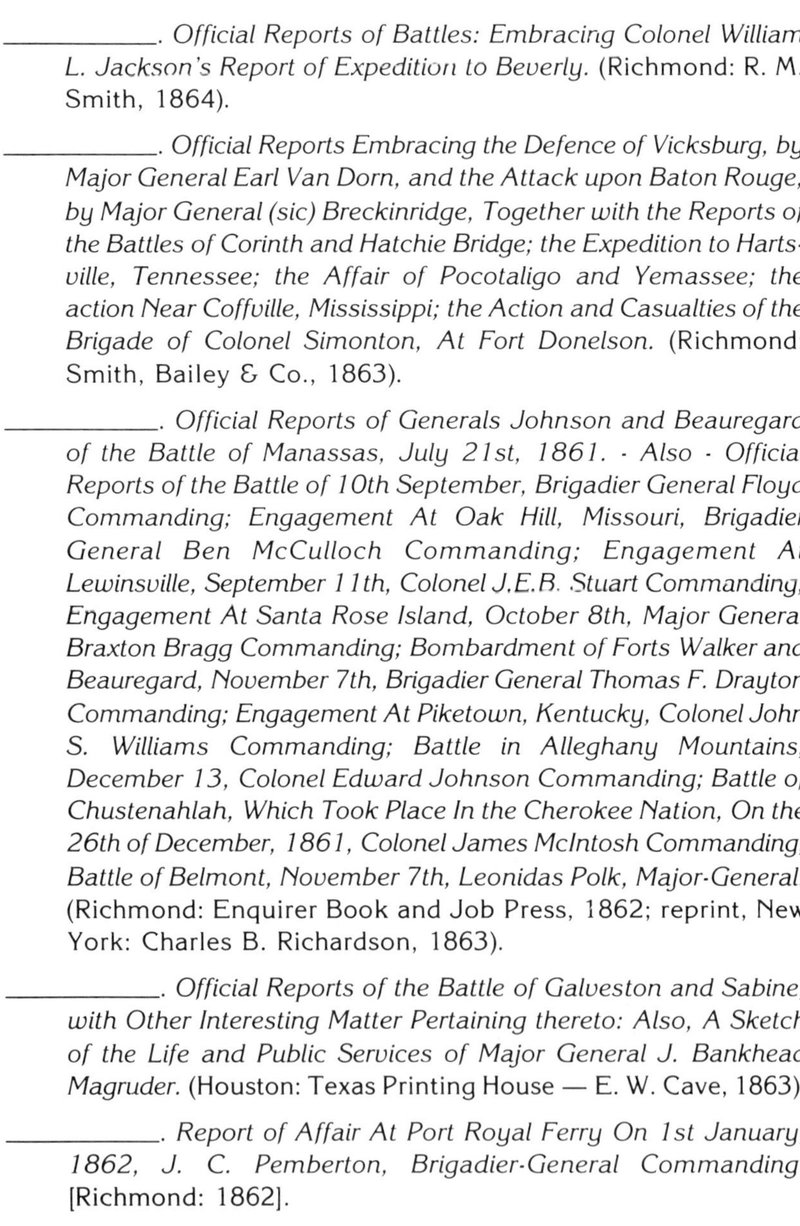

____________. *Official Reports of Battles: Embracing Colonel William L. Jackson's Report of Expedition to Beverly.* (Richmond: R. M. Smith, 1864).

____________. *Official Reports Embracing the Defence of Vicksburg, by Major General Earl Van Dorn, and the Attack upon Baton Rouge, by Major General (sic) Breckinridge, Together with the Reports of the Battles of Corinth and Hatchie Bridge; the Expedition to Harts-ville, Tennessee; the Affair of Pocotaligo and Yemassee; the action Near Coffville, Mississippi; the Action and Casualties of the Brigade of Colonel Simonton, At Fort Donelson.* (Richmond: Smith, Bailey & Co., 1863).

____________. *Official Reports of Generals Johnson and Beauregard of the Battle of Manassas, July 21st, 1861. - Also - Official Reports of the Battle of 10th September, Brigadier General Floyd Commanding; Engagement At Oak Hill, Missouri, Brigadier General Ben McCulloch Commanding; Engagement At Lewinsville, September 11th, Colonel J.E.B. Stuart Commanding; Engagement At Santa Rose Island, October 8th, Major General Braxton Bragg Commanding; Bombardment of Forts Walker and Beauregard, November 7th, Brigadier General Thomas F. Drayton Commanding; Engagement At Piketown, Kentucky, Colonel John S. Williams Commanding; Battle in Alleghany Mountains, December 13, Colonel Edward Johnson Commanding; Battle of Chustenahlah, Which Took Place In the Cherokee Nation, On the 26th of December, 1861, Colonel James McIntosh Commanding; Battle of Belmont, November 7th, Leonidas Polk, Major-General.* (Richmond: Enquirer Book and Job Press, 1862; reprint, New York: Charles B. Richardson, 1863).

____________. *Official Reports of the Battle of Galveston and Sabine, with Other Interesting Matter Pertaining thereto: Also, A Sketch of the Life and Public Services of Major General J. Bankhead Magruder.* (Houston: Texas Printing House — E. W. Cave, 1863).

____________. *Report of Affair At Port Royal Ferry On 1st January, 1862, J. C. Pemberton, Brigadier-General Commanding.* [Richmond: 1862].

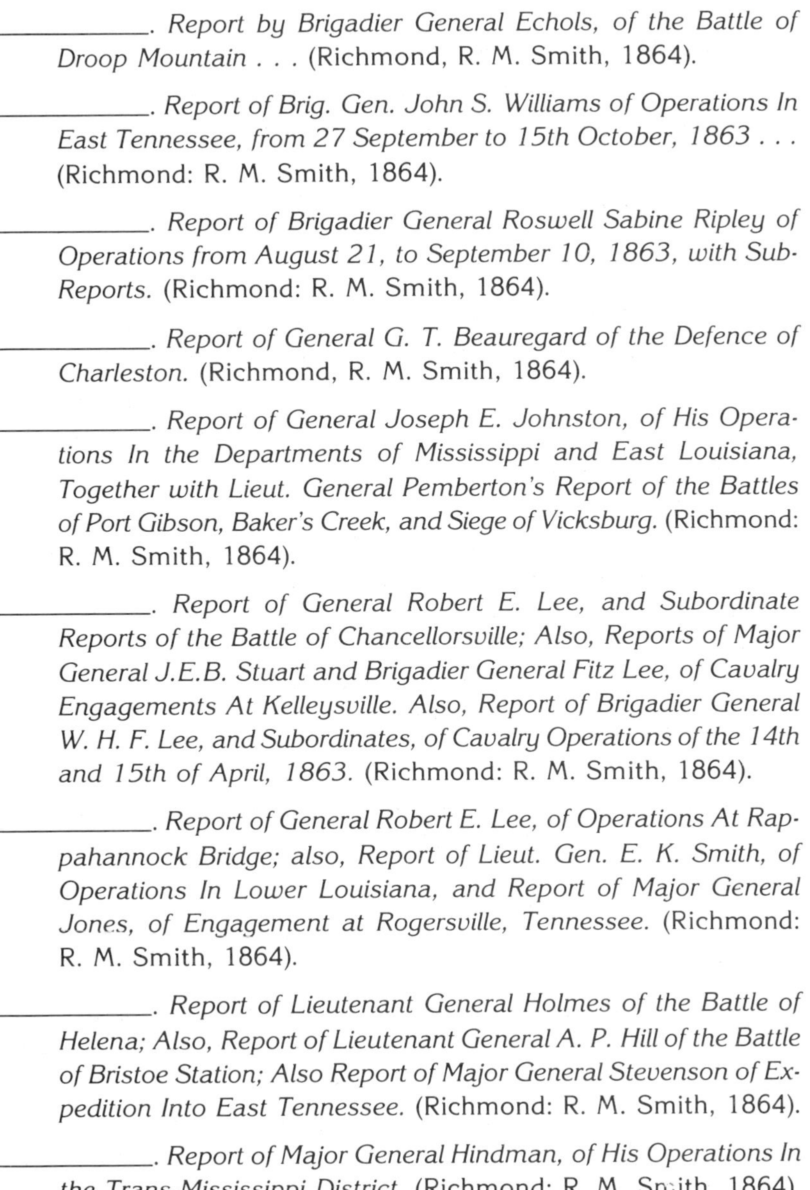

___________. *Report by Brigadier General Echols, of the Battle of Droop Mountain . . .* (Richmond, R. M. Smith, 1864).

___________. *Report of Brig. Gen. John S. Williams of Operations In East Tennessee, from 27 September to 15th October, 1863 . . .* (Richmond: R. M. Smith, 1864).

___________. *Report of Brigadier General Roswell Sabine Ripley of Operations from August 21, to September 10, 1863, with Sub-Reports.* (Richmond: R. M. Smith, 1864).

___________. *Report of General G. T. Beauregard of the Defence of Charleston.* (Richmond, R. M. Smith, 1864).

___________. *Report of General Joseph E. Johnston, of His Operations In the Departments of Mississippi and East Louisiana, Together with Lieut. General Pemberton's Report of the Battles of Port Gibson, Baker's Creek, and Siege of Vicksburg.* (Richmond: R. M. Smith, 1864).

___________. *Report of General Robert E. Lee, and Subordinate Reports of the Battle of Chancellorsville; Also, Reports of Major General J.E.B. Stuart and Brigadier General Fitz Lee, of Cavalry Engagements At Kelleysville. Also, Report of Brigadier General W. H. F. Lee, and Subordinates, of Cavalry Operations of the 14th and 15th of April, 1863.* (Richmond: R. M. Smith, 1864).

___________. *Report of General Robert E. Lee, of Operations At Rappahannock Bridge; also, Report of Lieut. Gen. E. K. Smith, of Operations In Lower Louisiana, and Report of Major General Jones, of Engagement at Rogersville, Tennessee.* (Richmond: R. M. Smith, 1864).

___________. *Report of Lieutenant General Holmes of the Battle of Helena; Also, Report of Lieutenant General A. P. Hill of the Battle of Bristoe Station; Also Report of Major General Stevenson of Expedition Into East Tennessee.* (Richmond: R. M. Smith, 1864).

___________. *Report of Major General Hindman, of His Operations In the Trans-Mississippi District.* (Richmond: R. M. Smith, 1864).

____________. *Report of Major General Leonidas Polk of the Battle of November 7, 1861.* (Richmond: 1861).

____________. *Report of Major General Loring, Battle of Baker's Creek, and Subsequent Movements of His Command.* (Richmond: R. M. Smith, 1864).

____________. *Report of the Engagement At Staunton River, June 25th, 1864.* [n.p.: 1864]

____________. *Report of the Secretary of War . . . 14th Dec., 1861; August 12, 1862; January 3, 1863; Nov. 26, 1863; April 28, 1864; November 3, 1864.* (Richmond: 1861-1864).

____________. *Reports of the Operations of the Army of Northern Virginia, from June 1862, and Including the Battle At Fredericksburg, Dec., 13, 1862,* 2 vol. (Richmond, R. M. Smith, 1864).

____________. *Response of Secretary of War, to the Resolutions of the Senate, Adopted December 5th, 1864, Respecting Operations Under the Act of 6th February, 1864 . . . December 10, 1864.* [Richmond: 1864].

____________. *Supplemental Report of the Secretary of War . . . March 17th, 1862.* [Richmond: 1862].

B. MISCELLANEOUS CONFEDERATE SOURCES PUBLISHED BY THE UNITED STATES GOVERNMENT

Bethel, Elizabeth, comp. *War Department Collection of Confederate Records,* NARS PI 101. Washington, D.C.: National Archives, 1957.

Confederate Congress. *Journals.* U.S. Senate Document Number 234, vol. 25-31 (58th Congress, 2nd Session); microfiche on 76 fiche, Bethesda, MD: University Publications of America, 1990.

Confederate States of America. War Department. *Local Designations of Confederate Organizations,* comp. by Marcus J. Wright. Washington, D.C.: 1876.

____________. *Special Orders of the Adjutant and Inspector General's Office*, 2 vols. Washington, D.C.: U.S. War Department. Record & Pension Office, 1889-1904. [Never compiled by the Confederate government].

Ryan, Carmelita S., comp. *Preliminary Inventory of the Treasury Department Collection of Confederate Records (Record Group 365).* Washington, D.C.: National Archives, 1967.

U.S. Adjutant General's Office. *List of Synonyms of Organizations In the Volunteer Service of the United States During 1861-1865*, comp. by John T. Fallon. Washington, D.C.: 1885.

U.S. Army. War Records Publication Office. *Records of the Confederate Armies in Possession of the Southern Historical Society at Richmond Virginia.* Washington, D.C.: 1880.

U.S. National Archives. *Confederate States Army Casualties: Lists and Narrative Reports, 1861-65*, comp. by David Gibon. Washington, D.C.: 1971.

U.S. Naval War Records Office. *Uniform and Dress of the Navy of the Confederate States.* Washington, D.C.: 1898.

U.S. Record and Pension Office. Confederate States. *Executive and Congressional Directory of Confederate States, 1861-65*, comp. from official records. Washington, D.C.: 1899.

____________. Ordnance Museum. *Catalogue of Rebel Flags Captured by Union Troops, Since April 9, 1861, Deposited In the Ordnance Museum, War Department.* Washington, D.C.: 18____.

U.S. War Department. *Memorandum Relative to the General Officers Appointed by the President In the Armies of the Confederate States, 1861-1865.* Washington, D.C.: 1905.

U.S. War Records Office. *List of Staff Officers of the Confederate States Army, 1861-1865.* Washington, D.C.: 1891.

APPENDIX V

Civil War Map Sources Outside The *Rebellion Records*

Antietam Battlefield Board. *Atlas of the Battlefield of Antietam.* Washington, D.C.: 1904; 2nd ed., 1909.

Bearss, Edwin C. *Troop Movement Maps: Battle of First Manassas and Engagement At Blackburn's Ford, July 18 & 21, 1861.* Prince William and Fairfax Counties, VA: Manassas National Battlefield Park, 1960.

Chickamauga and Chattanooga National Park Commission. *Atlas of Battlefields of Chickamauga, Chattanooga and Vicinity With Descriptions of Plates and Positions of Troops.* Washington, D.C.: U.S. Government Printing Office, 1896-1897; reprinted with additional position maps, 1901. Found also in House Document 513, 46th Congress, 2nd Session.

Hotchkiss, Jedediah. *Battlefield of Virginia — Chancellorsville: Embracing the Operations of the Army of Northern Virginia from the First Battle of Fredericksburg to the Death of Lieutenant General Jackson.* NY: D. Van Nostrand, 1867.

Phillips, Phlip Lee. *Virginia Cartography, A Biographical Description.* Washington, D.C.: 1896.

Stephenson, Richard W., comp. *Civil War Maps: An Annotated List of Maps and Atlases In the Map Collections of the Library of Congress.* Washington, D.C.: Library of Congress, 1961; reprint, Westport, CT: Greenwood Press, 1979.

____________. *Civil War Maps: Includes Descriptions of 2,240 Maps and Charts and 76 Atlases and Sketchbooks, Chiefly Housed In the Library of Congress, Geographic and Map Division, Also Cites 162 Maps from 28 Manuscript Collections*, rev. ed. Washington, D.C.: Library of Congress, 1989.

U.S. Army. Adjutant General's Office and Surgeon-General. *Chronological Summary of Engagements and Battles with Maps from the Medical and Surgical History of the War of the Rebellion, 1861-1865.* Philadelphia: 1880.

U.S. Department of Commerce. National Oceanic and Atmosphere Administration, National Ocean Survey. Physical Science Services Branch. Map Library. *National Ocean Survey Cartobibliography: Civil War Collection.* Rockville, MD: 1980.

U.S. Department of the Interior. *A Bibliography of Maps of Civil War Battlefield Areas*, comp. by Irwin Gottschall, Geological Survey Circular 462. Washington, D.C.: 1962.

U.S. Library of Congress. Map Division. *The Hotchkiss Map Collection: A List of Manuscript Maps, Many of the Civil War Period, Prepared by Major Jed. Hotchkiss and Other Manuscript and Annotated Maps In His Possession*, ed. by Clara Egli Le Gear. Washington, D.C.: 1951.

U.S. National Archives and Records Service. *A Guide to Civil War Maps In the National Archives*, comp. by Charlotte M. Ashby and rev. by William J. Heynen. Washington, D.C.: 1964; rev. ed. 1986.

U.S. War Department. Office of the Chief of Engineers. *Military Maps Illustrating the Operations of the Armies of the Potomac & James, May 4th 1864 to April 9th 1865 Including Battlefields of the Wilderness, Spottsylvania, Northanna, Totopotomay, Cold Harbor, the Siege of Petersburg and Richmond, Battlefields of Five Forks, Jetersville & Sailor's Creek, Highbridge & Farmsville & Appomattox Court-House.* Washington, D.C.: 1867.

Virginia Historical Society. *Confederate Engineers' Maps: Jeremy Francis Gilmer Collection.* Richmond: 1989.

Appendix VI

Rebellion Records **Reprints**

A. *OR-ARMIES*

Church of Jesus Christ of Latter-Day Saints. Genealogical Library. Microfilm of the *OR-Armies*, organized by reel numbers, 845.306-845.426 and *OR-Armies, General Index*, 430.054.

U.S. Congress. See Appendix VII.

__________. Congressional Information Service. Microfiche of Superintendent of Documents publications including the *OR-Armies*, *OR-Atlas* and *OR-Navies*. Washington, D.C.: 1970s.

__________. *War of Rebellion, Compilation of Official Records of Union and Confederate Armies.* War Department classification number W45.5.

__________. . . . *General Index and Additions and Corrections.* War Department classification number W45.6.

__________. *Battles, War of the Rebellion.* Washington, D.C.: 1899. This is an index to battles from Series I of the *OR.*

__________. *War of the Rebellion: A Compilation of the Official Records of the Union and Confederate Armies*, ed. by Robert N. Scott *et al.*, 70 vols. in 128 parts. Washington, D.C.: 1881-1901. For holding libraries see: OCLC 12241509.

__________. Republished in 128, 16 mm microfilm reels, Microfilm Number 262. Washington, D.C.: National Archives and Records Service, 1959.

__________. Facsimile republication. Harrisburg, PA: Historical Times, Inc., Morningside House and Broadfoot Publishing Company, 1971-1972; republication, 1985 and 1992.

__________. Republished in 35 microfiche film cards. Chicago: Encyclopaedia Britannica Co., Library Microbook Library of American Civilization Resources, Inc., 1974.

__________. Republished in 70 microfilm reels. Wooster, OH: Micro Photo Division, Bell & Howell, 1978.

__________. *General Index and Additions and Corrections*, 1902 ed. Harrisburg, PA: National Historical Society, 1972.

B. *OR-NAVIES*

U.S. Navy Department. *Official Records of the Union and Confederate Navies In the Rebellion*, ed. by Richard Bush et al., 31 vols. Washington, D.C.: 1894-1927. For holding libraries see OCLC 7766091 or OCLC 16746889.

__________. 31 reels, 16 mm Microfilm 275. Washington, D.C.: National Archives and Records Service, 1968.

__________. Republished in 39 microfiche film cards. Chicago: Encyclopaedia Britannica Co., Library Microbook Library of American Civilization Resources, Inc., 1972.

__________. Reprint. NY: Arno, 1976.

__________. Republished in 4 microfilm reels. Wooster, OH: Micro Photo Division, Bell & Howell, 1978.

__________. Reprint. Harrisburg, PA: National Historical Society, 1987.

__________. *General Index.* Washington, D.C.: 1927; reprint, NY: Antiquarian Press, 1961.

U.S. Superintendent of Documents. *Official Records of the Union and Confederate Navies In the War of Rebellion*, 31 vols. Navy Department classification number N16.6.

C. *OR-ATLAS*

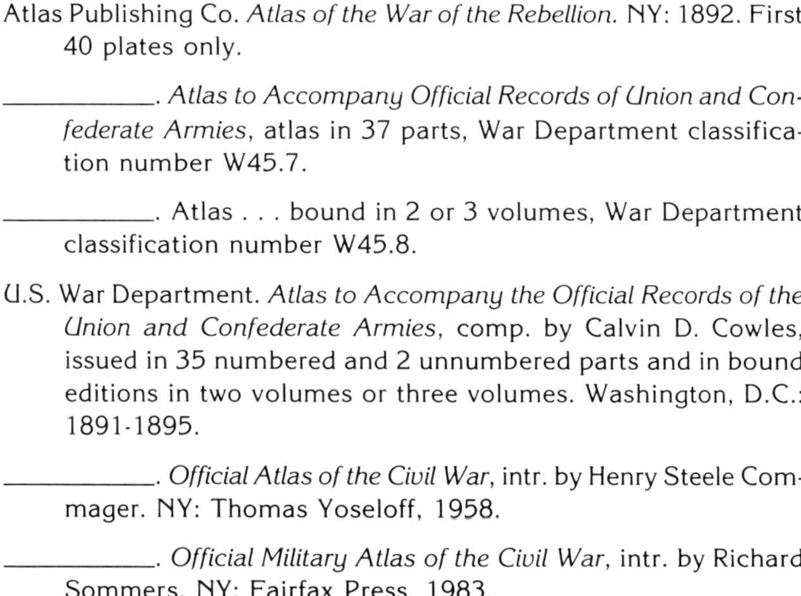

Atlas Publishing Co. *Atlas of the War of the Rebellion.* NY: 1892. First 40 plates only.

____________. *Atlas to Accompany Official Records of Union and Confederate Armies*, atlas in 37 parts, War Department classification number W45.7.

____________. Atlas . . . bound in 2 or 3 volumes, War Department classification number W45.8.

U.S. War Department. *Atlas to Accompany the Official Records of the Union and Confederate Armies*, comp. by Calvin D. Cowles, issued in 35 numbered and 2 unnumbered parts and in bound editions in two volumes or three volumes. Washington, D.C.: 1891-1895.

____________. *Official Atlas of the Civil War*, intr. by Henry Steele Commager. NY: Thomas Yoseloff, 1958.

____________. *Official Military Atlas of the Civil War*, intr. by Richard Sommers. NY: Fairfax Press, 1983.

Appendix VII

Rebellion Records In The House Miscellaneous Documents — A Correlation Chart

Researchers are typically familiar with the *Rebellion Records* as bound and numbered by the U.S. War and Navy Departments. Often overlooked, however, is their availability in government document collections. From 1882 through 1927 the *Rebellion Records* were included in House Miscellaneous Documents, identified by Superintendent of Document serial numbers. The major disadvantage of these sets is that the individual books are "scattered" throughout 45 years of the House Miscellaneous Documents making it cumbersome to find specific books.

To facilitate finding and using the *Rebellion Records* in these government document holdings, a chart correlating the War and Navy Department designations of each book with the House Miscellaneous Document Report Number is provided below. [Many government depository libraries now have these documents available on microfiche.]

*The House Miscellaneous Document Number listed in the right column below is needed to expedite location of the required volume within the government document holdings. It specifies, in order, the Congress, Session, Serial Number, Document Number and Part Number, if any.

The U.S. War and Navy Department designations in the left column indicate, in order, the volume and part (if any) followed, in parentheses, by the Serial number assigned to the book.

RECORDS, ARMIES

U.S. War Dept. Designation			House Misc. Document Number				
Series I							
1		(1)	52d,	2nd,	3112,	40	
2		(2)	52d,	2nd,	3113,	41	
3		(3)	52d,	2nd,	3114,	42	
4		(4)	47th,	1st,	3115,	43	
5		(5)	47th,	1st,	2053,	54	
6		(6)	47th,	1st,	2058,	63	
7		(7)	47th,	1st,	2063,	67	
8		(8)	47th,	2nd,	2122,	27	
9		(9)	47th,	2nd,	2128,	41	
10,	1	(10)	48th,	1st,	2225,	26	
10,	2	(11)	48th,	1st,	2229,	32	
11,	1	(12)	48th,	1st,	2240,	65,	1
11,	2	(13)	48th,	1st,	2241,	65,	2
11,	3	(14)	48th,	1st,	2242,	65,	3
12,	1	(15)	48th,	2nd,	2322,	37,	1
12,	2	(16)	48th,	2nd,	2323,	37,	2
12,	2d suppl	(17)	49th,	2nd,	2490,	54	
12,	3	(18)	48th,	2nd,	2324,	37,	3
13		(19)	49th,	1st,	2408,	21	
14		(20)	49th,	1st,	2409,	22	
15		(21)	49th,	1st,	2416,	164	
16,	1	(22)	49th,	1st,	2419,	273	
16,	2	(23)	49th,	1st,	2421,	338	
17,	1	(24)	49th,	1st,	2425,	371	
17,	2	(25)	49th,	2nd,	2489,	53	
18		(26)	50th,	1st,	2571,	325	
19,	1	(27)	50th,	1st,	2572,	338	
19,	2	(28)	50th,	1st,	2573,	339	
20,	1	(29)	50th,	1st,	2574,	341	
20,	2	(30)	50th,	1st,	2575,	342	
21		(31)	50th,	1st,	2577,	387	

U.S. War Dept. Designation *(cont'd.)*			House Misc. Document Number *(cont'd.)*				
Series I							
22,	1	(32)	50th,	1st,	2580,	585	
22,	2	(33)	50th,	2nd,	2656,	60	
23,	1	(34)	50th,	2nd,	2659,	113	
23,	2	(35)	50th,	2nd,	2660,	129	
24,	1	(36)	51st,	1st,	2761,	4	
24,	2	(37)	51st,	1st,	2762,	5	
24,	3	(38)	51st,	1st,	2763,	6	
25,	1	(39)	51st,	1st,	2766,	44	
25,	2	(40)	51st,	1st,	2767,	45	
26,	1	(41)	51st,	1st,	2769,	105	
26,	2	(42)	51st,	1st,	2770,	106	
27,	1	(43)	51st,	1st,	2771,	146	
27,	2	(44)	51st,	1st,	2772,	147	
27,	3	(45)	51st,	1st,	2773,	148	
28,	1	(46)	51st,	1st,	2778,	223	
28,	2	(47)	51st,	1st,	2781,	228	
29,	1	(48)	51st,	1st,	2789,	240	
29,	2	(49)	51st,	1st,	2790,	241	
30,	1	(50)	51st,	1st,	2792,	245	
30,	2	(51)	51st,	1st,	2793,	246	
30,	3	(52)	51st,	1st,	2794,	247	
30,	4	(53)	51st,	1st,	2795,	248	
31,	1	(54)	51st,	2nd,	2870,	12	
31,	2	(55)	51st,	2nd,	2871,	13	
31,	3	(56)	51st,	2nd,	2872,	14	
32,	1	(57)	51st,	2nd,	2873,	76	
32,	2	(58)	51st,	2nd,	2874,	77	
32,	3	(59)	51st,	2nd,	2875,	78	
33		(60)	52nd,	1st,	2961,	12	
34,	1	(61)	52nd,	1st,	2962,	13,	1
34,	2	(62)	52nd,	1st,	2963,	13,	2

U.S. War Dept. Designation *(cont'd.)*			House Misc. Document Number				
Series I							
34,	3	(63)	52nd,	1st,	2964,	13,	3
34,	4	(64)	52nd,	1st,	2965,	13,	4
35,	1	(65)	52nd	1st,	2966,	14,	1
35,	2	(66)	52nd,	1st,	2967,	14,	2
36,	1	(67)	52nd,	1st,	2968,	15,	1
36,	2	(68)	52nd,	1st,	2969,	15,	2
36,	3	(69)	52nd,	1st,	2970,	15,	3
37,	1	(70)	52nd,	1st,	2971,	16,	1
37,	2	(71)	52nd,	1st,	2972,	16,	2
38,	1	(72)	52nd,	1st,	2980,	48,	1
38,	2	(73)	52nd,	1st,	2981,	48,	2
38,	3	(74)	52nd,	1st,	2982,	48,	3
38,	4	(75)	52nd,	1st,	2983,	48,	4
38,	5	(76)	52nd,	1st,	2984,	48,	5
39,	1	(77)	52nd,	1st,	2993,	233,	1
39,	2	(78)	52nd,	1st,	2994,	233,	2
39,	3	(79)	52nd,	1st,	2995,	233,	3
40,	1	(80)	52nd,	1st,	3004,	338,	1
40,	2	(81)	52nd,	1st,	3005,	338,	2
40,	3	(82)	52nd,	1st,	3006,	338,	3
41,	1	(83)	52nd,	2nd,	3119,	96,	1
41,	2	(84)	52nd,	2nd,	3120,	96,	2
41,	3	(85)	52nd,	2nd,	3121,	96,	3
41,	4	(86)	52nd,	2nd,	3122,	96,	4
42,	1	(87)	53rd,	1st,	3152,	9,	1
42,	2	(88)	53rd,	1st,	3153,	9,	2
42,	3	(89)	53rd,	1st,	3154,	9,	3
43,	1	(90)	53rd,	2nd,	3225,	55,	1
43,	2	(91)	53rd,	2nd,	3236,	55,	2
44		(92)	53rd,	2nd,	3240,	97	
45,	1	(93)	53rd,	2nd,	3244,	121,	1

U.S. War Dept. Designation *(cont'd.)*			House Misc. Document Number *(cont'd.)*				
Series I							
45,	2	(94)	53rd,	2nd,	3245,	121,	2
46,	1	(95)	53rd,	2nd,	3261,	208,	1
46,	2	(96)	53rd,	2nd,	3262,	208,	2
46,	3	(97)	53rd,	2nd,	3263,	208,	3
47,	1	(98)	54th,	1st,	3409,	37,	1
47,	2	(99)	54th,	1st,	3410,	37,	2
47,	3	(100)	54th,	1st,	3411,	37,	3
48,	1	(101)	54th,	1st,	3436,	369,	1
48,	2	(102)	54th,	1st,	3437,	369,	2
49,	1	(103)	54th,	2nd,	3532,	251,	1
49,	2	(104)	54th,	2nd,	3533,	251,	2
50,	1	(105)	54th,	1st,	3583,	59,	1
50,	2	(106)	54th,	1st,	3584,	59,	2
51,	1	(107)	54th,	1st,	3585,	95,	1
51,	2	(108)	54th,	1st,	3586,	95,	2
52,	1	(109)	54th,	2nd,	3684,	288,	1
52,	2	(110)	54th,	2nd,	3685,	288,	2
53		(111)	54th,	2nd,	3686,	476	
54		(112) not published					
55		(113) not published					
Series II							
1		(114)	54th,	3rd,	3787,	65,	1
2		(115)	54th,	3rd,	3788,	66,	2
3		(116)	54th,	3rd,	3789,	67,	3
4		(117)	55th,	3rd,	3790,	284,	4
5		(118)	55th,	3rd,	3791,	311,	5
6		(119)	55th,	3rd,	3792,	312,	6
7		(120)	55th,	3rd,	3793,	313,	7
8		(121)	55th,	3rd,	3794,	314,	8

Series III

1	(122)	56th,	1st,	3962,	117,	1
2	(123)	56th,	1st,	3963,	118,	2
3	(124)	56th,	1st,	3964,	287,	3
4	(125)	56th,	1st,	3965,	496,	4
5	(126)	56th,	1st,	3966,	553,	5

Series IV

1	(127)	56th,	1st,	3967,	579,	1
2	(128)	56th,	1st,	3968,	658,	2
3	(129)	56th,	1st,	3969,	678,	3

GENERAL INDEX (130)	56th,	2nd,	4209,	558	
OFFICIAL RECORDS,	52nd,	1st,	2998,	261,	1
ATLAS	52nd,	1st,	2998,	261,	2

OFFICIAL RECORDS, NAVIES

U.S. Naval Dept. Designation	House Misc. Document Number			
Series I				
1	53rd,	3rd,	3332,	58
2	54th,	1st,	3408,	36
3	54th,	1st,	3440,	379
4	54th,	2nd,	3515,	40
5	55th,	1st,	3573,	60
6	55th,	2nd,	3682,	262
7	55th,	2nd,	3683,	559

U.S. Naval Dept. Designation *(cont'd.)*	House Misc. Document Number *(cont'd.)*			
Series I				
8	55th,	3rd,	3823,	286
9	56th,	1st,	3960,	115
10	56th,	1st,	3961,	735
11	56th,	2nd,	4160,	314
12	56th,	2nd,	4161,	542
13	57th,	1st,	4352,	283
14	57th,	1st,	4353,	681
15	57th,	2nd,	4497,	156
16	57th,	2nd,	4498,	477
17	58th,	2nd,	4704,	404
18	58th,	2nd,	4705,	750
19	58th,	3rd,	4889,	459
20	59th,	1st,	5025,	341
21	59th,	2nd,	5148,	25
22	60th,	2nd,	5451,	1024
23	60th,	2nd,	5742,	986
24	61st,	2nd,	5743,	987
25	61st,	3rd,	5974,	1017
26	62nd,	2nd,	6221,	179
27	62nd,	3rd,	6407,	983
Series II				
1	67th,	2nd,	8015,	253
2	67th,	2nd,	8016,	254
3	67th,	2nd,	8017,	316
GENERAL INDEX	69th,	1st,	8603,	113

APPENDIX VIII

Index To Principal Events In The *Official Records*

1 Seizure of United States forts, etc.; vessels fired upon by State troops; expeditions for the relief of Forts Pickens and Sumter; bombardment and evacuation of Fort Sumter.

2 Sewell's Point, Aquia Creek, Philippi, Big Bethel, Falling Waters, Rich Mountain, Blackburn's Ford, Bull Run (1st), the Miles Court of Inquiry.

3 Camp Jackson, Booneville, Carthage, Blue Mills, Wilson's Creek, Lexington, Fredericktown, Springfield, Belmont.

4 San Augustine Springs; advance of Confederates into Kentucky; Columbus, Paducah, Barboursville, Camp Wildcat, Ivy Mountain; revolt of Unionists in East Tennessee; burning of Hampton; Hatteras Inlet.

5 Cross-Lanes, Carnifix Ferry, Cheat Mountain; arrest of members of Maryland Legislature; Rommey, Greenbrier River, Kanawha and New Rivers, Ball's Bluff, Camp Alleghany, Dranesville, Hancock.

6 Port Royal, Jacksonville, Fort Pulaski, Pensacola, Forts Jackson and Saint Philip, New Orleans, the Lovell Court of Inquiry.

7 Rowlett's Station, Prestonburg, Logan's Cross-Roads or Mill Springs, Forts Henry and Donelson.

8 Round Mountain, Chusto-Talasah, Chustenahlah, Mount Zion Church, Roan's Tan Yard, New Madrid, Island No. 10, Pea Ridge.

9 Monitor and Merrimac, Roanoake Island, New Berne, Fort Macon, South Mills, Tranter's Creek, Valverde, Glorieta, "The California Column."

10-11 Cumberland Gap, Pittsburg Landing or Shiloh, "Railroad Raid," Corinth, Fort Pillow, Memphis, Chattanooga.

12-13-14 Yorktown, Williamsburg, West Point, Fort Darling, Hanover Court-House, Fair Oaks or Seven Pines, Stuart's Raid, Seven Days' Battles (including Oak Grove, Mechanicsville, Gaines' Mill, Garnett's and Golding's Farms, Peach Orchard, Savage Station, White Oak Swamp Bridge, Glendale, (Turkey Bridge, Malvern Hill).

15-16-17-18 Kernstown, McDowell, Princeton, Front Royal, Middletown, Winchester, Cross Keys, Port Republic, Cedar Mountain, Rappahannock Station, Kettle Run, Thoroughfare Gap, Gainesville, Groveton, Bull Run (2nd), Chantilly, the McDowell Court of Inquiry, the Porter Commission and Court-Martial and the Julius White Commission.

19 Saint Charles, Hill's Plantation, Kirksville, Independence, Lone Jack, Fort Ridgely, Newtonia, Old Fort Wayne, Clark's Mill.

20 Secessionville, Simmons' Bluff, Tampa, Saint John's Bluff, Fort McAllister, Jacksonville, Charleston Harbor.

21 Natchez, Vicksburg, Baton Rouge, Donaldsville, Sabine Pass, Galveston, Port Hudson, Georgia Landing, Bisland, Irish Bend, Bayou Vermillion, the Sibley and Grant Courts-Martial.

22-23 Cumberland Gap, Morgan's (1st) Kentucky Raid, Murfreesboro, Richmond, Munfordville, Perryville or Chaplin Hills, the Burll Commission and the T. T. Crittenden Court of Inquiry.

24-25	Iuka, Corith, Coffeeville, Holly Springs, Jackson, Parker's Cross-Roads, Chickasaw Bluffs, Arkansas Post, the Van Dorn Court of Inquiry.
26	Plymouth, Kinston, White Hall, Goldsborough, Deserted House, Fort Anderson, Washington, Suffolk.
27-28	South Mountain, Crampton's Pass, Harper's Ferry, Antietam, Kanawha Valley, Stuart's Raid, the Harper's Ferry Commission and the Fredericksburg Court of Inquiry.
29-30	Hartsville, Carter's Raid, Morgan's (2nd) Kentucky Raid, Mutiny of the Anderson Cavalry, Stone's River, Wheeler's Raid.
31	Fredericksburg, Dumfries, "Mud March."
32-33	Cane Hill, Praire Grove, Springfield, Hartville, Cape Cirardeau, Big Mound, Dead Buffalo Lake, Stony Lake, Cabin Creek, Helena, Honey Springs, Bayou Fourche, Little Rock, White Stone Hill, Quantrill's Raid, Devil's Backbone, Shelby's Raid, Baxter Springs, Pine Bluff.
34-35	Thompson's Station, Vaught's Hill, Pegram's Raid, Brentwood, Wheeler's Railroad Raid, Franklin, Streight's Raid, Everett's Raid, Sanders' Raid, Hines' Raid, Tullahoma Campaign, Morgan's Ohio Raid, Scott's Raid.
36-37-38	Yazoo Pass, Steele's Bayou, Grierson's Raid, Grand Gulf, Snyder's Mill, Port Gibson, Raymond, Jackson, Champion's Hill, Big Black River Bridge, Vicksburg, Milliken's Bend, Goodrich's Landing.
39-40	Kelly's Ford, Imboden's Raid, Jones' Raid, Marye's and Salem Heights, Chancellorsville, Stoneman's Raid.
41-42	Plains Store, Port Hudson, La Fourche Crossing, Donaldsonville, Cox's Plantation, Sabine Pass, Stirling's Plantation, Teche, Rio Grande.
43-44-45	Brandy Station, Winchester, Upperville, Hanover, Gettysburg, Williamsport, Boonsborough, Falling Waters, Shepherdstown, Wapping Heights, New York Draft Riots, the Milroy and Tyler Court of Inquiry.

46-47	Grimball's Landing, Morris Island, Battery Wagner, Fort Sumter, Charleston, Fort Brooke.
48-49	Averell's Raid, Auburn, Bristoe Station, Buckland Mills, Droop Mountain, Rappahannock Station, Kelly's Ford, Mine Run, the Charlestown Court of Inquiry.
50-51	Chickamauga, Knoxville, Bountsville, Blue Springs, Wheeler and Roddey's Raid, Chalmers' Raid, Bogue.
52-53	Chitto Creek, the McCook, Crittenden and Negley Court of Inquiry.
54-55-56	Reopening of Tennessee River, Wauhatchie, Collierville, Campbell's Station, Knoxville (Ft. Sanders), Lookout Mountain, Missionary Ridge, Ringgold Gap, Bean's Station, Mossy Creek, the Schurz and Heckert Court of Inquiry and the McLawn Court-Martial.
57	Dandridge Athens, Fair Garden.
58	Meridian, Okolona, Dalton.
59	Fort Pillow.
60	New Berne, Morton's Ford, Gilmor's Raid, Custer's Raid, Kilpatrick's Raid.
61-62-63 -64	Red River, Sabine Cross-Roads, Pleasant Hill, Blair's Landing, Monett's Ferry, Mansura, Yellow Bayou, Camden, Elkin's Ferry, Poison Spring, Marks' Mills, Jenkins' Ferry, Old River Lake.
65-66	Charleston Harbor, Olustee or Ocean Pond, Marianna.
67-68-69	Wilderness, Spotsylvania, North Anna, Totopotomoy, Haw's Shop, Old Church, Shady Grove, Cold Harbor, Bethesda Church, Yellow Tavern, Trevilian Station, Saint Mary's Church, Ram Albemarle, Kautz's Raids, Port Walthall, Chester Station, Fort Clifton, Swift Creek, Proctor's Creek, Drewry's Bluff, Bermuda Hundred, Wilson's Wharf, Petersburg, the Gilmore and Barton Courts of Inquiry.

70-71	Cloyd's Mountain, New Market, Piedmont, Lynchburg, Monocacy, Fort Stevens, Snicker's Ferry, Berry's Ford, Stephenson's Depot, Winchester, Chambersburg, Cumberland.
72-73-74 -75-76	Rocky Face Ridge, Dalton, Resaca, Adairsville, New Hope Church, Pickett's Mills, Dallas, Marietta, Kenesaw Mountain, Kolb's Farm, Rousseau's Raid, Peach Tree Creek, Atlanta, Garrard's Raids, Ezra Church, Utoy Creek, McCook's Raid, Stoneman's Raid, Wheeler's Raid, Kilpatrick's Raid, Jonesborough, Lovejoy's Station.
77-78-79	Morgan's Kentucky Raid, Brice's Cross-Roads, Tupelo, Oxford, Mobile Bay, Memphis, Forrest's Raids, Allatoona, Decatur, Johnsonville, Bull's Gap.
80-81-82	Richmond, Petersburg, Jerusalem Plank Road, Strawberry Plains or First Deep Bottom, The Mine, the Court of Inquiry on the Mine Explosion.
83-84-85 -86	Tahkahokuty Mountain, Price's Missouri Expedition (incl. Ft. Davidson, Glasgow, Lexington, Little Blue, Independence, Big Blue, Westport, Marais des Cygnes, Little Osage River, Charlot and Newtonia), Adobe Ft., Sand Creek.
87-88-89	Richmond, Petersburg, Deep Bottom (2nd) Weldon Railroad, Reams' Station, Chaffin's Farm, Poplar Spring Church, Darbytown Road, Boydton Plank Road, Fort Fisher (1st).
90-91	Cedarville, Smithfield Crossing, Berryville, Opequon or Winchester, Fisher's Hill, Tom's Brook, Cedar Creek.
92	Griswoldville, Buck Head Creek, Honey Hill, Waynesborough, Savannah, Fort McAllister.
93-94	Columbia, Spring Hill, Franklin (TN), Murfreesborough, Lyon's Raid, Nashville, Marion, Saltville, Verona, Egypt, Franklin (MS), the Hodge Court of Inquiry.

95-96-97 Richmond, Petersburg, Ft. Fisher (2nd), Hatcher's Run, Waynesborough, Ft. Stedman, Lewis' Farm, White Oak Road, Dinwiddie Court-House, Five Forks, Sutherland's Station, Amelia Springs, Sailor's Creek, Rice's Station, High Bridge, Farmville, Appomattox Court-House, Surrender of Lee's Army, Review of the Army of the Potomac.

98-99-100 Columbia, Charleston, Wilmington, Kinston or Wise's Forks, Monroe's Cross-Roads, Averasborough, Bentonville, Goldsborough, Raleigh, Durham Station [surrender of Johnston's Army), Surrender of Confederate Troops in Florida, Review of Sherman's Army.

101-102 Rio Grande Border, Powder River Expedition, Loss of the Sultana, Surrender of Kirby Smith's Army and Jeff Thompson's Command.

103-104 Spanish Ft., Ft. Blakely, Mobile, Stoneman's Raid, Wilson's Raid, Surrender of Taylor's Army, Capture of Jefferson Davis.

105-106 The Showalter Party, the Party, the California Column, Bear River.

107-108 Supplement to Volumes 1, 2, 4, 5, 9, 11, 12, 18, 19, 21, 25, 27, 29, 33, 36, 37, 40, 42, 43, 46.

109-110 Supplement to Volumes 1, 4, 6, 7, 10, 15, 16, 17, 20, 23, 24, 26, 30, 31, 32, 38, 39, 45, 49.

111 Supplement to Volumes 1, 3, 4, 6, 8, 9, 13, 14, 15, 22, 26, 28, 34, 35, 41, 44, 47, 48, 50.

112-113 (Volumes 112 and 113 were reserved by the *OR-Armies* editors but never published.)

114 The Texas Surrender, Feb. 5-Nov. 1, 1861; Earlier captures and arrests, and measures of pacification in Missouri, Mar.13, 1861-Jan. 12, 1862; Union policy of repression in Maryland, Apr. 20, 1861-Nov. 29, 1862; Military treatment of captured and fugitive slaves, Mar. 18, 1861-May 10, 1862; Confederate policy of repression in East Tennessee, May 25, 1861-Apr. 21, 1862.

115 Treatment of suspected and disloyal persons, North and South, 1861-1863.

116 Correspondence, orders, etc., relating to prisoners of war and state, Feb. 19, 1861-June 12, 1862.

117 Correspondence, orders, etc., relating to prisoners of war and state, June 13-Nov. 30, 1862.

118 Correspondence, orders, etc., relating to prisoners of war and state, Dec. 1, 1862-June 10, 1863. Includes the Vallandigham Commission.

119 Correspondence, orders, etc., relating to prisoners of war and state, June 11, 1863-Mar. 31, 1864.

120 Correspondence, orders, etc., relating to prisoners of war and state, Apr. 1-Dec. 31, 1864. Includes documents relating to the Orders of American Knights and kindred organizations.

121 Correspondence, orders, etc., relating to prisoners of war and state, Jan. 1, 1865, to the end. Includes documents relating to the Order of American Knights, the trials of Wirz and the assassins of Lincoln and Seward, and the imprisonment of Jefferson Davis and other topics.

122 Correspondence, orders, reports and returns, Nov. 1, 1860-Mar. 31, 1862.

123 Correspondence, orders, reports and returns, Apr. 1-Dec. 31, 1862.

124 Correspondence, orders, reports and returns, Jan. 1-Dec. 31, 1863.

125 Correspondence, orders, reports and returns, Jan. 1, 1864-Apr. 30, 1865.

126 Correspondence, orders, reports and returns, May 1, 1865, to the end.

127 Correspondence, orders, reports and returns, Dec. 20, 1860-June 30, 1862.

128 Correspondence, orders, reports and returns, July 1, 1862-Dec. 31, 1863.

129 Correspondence, orders, reports and returns, Jan. 1, 1864, to the end.

130 General index to the entire work, with an appendix containing additions and corrections of errors discovered in the several volumes after their publication. It also includes "Special Compilations" containing (1) a synopsis of the contents of volumes; (2) a special index for the principal armies, army corps, military divisions and departments, and (3) a table showing volumes pertaining to contemporaneous operations.

Appendix IX

Index To Principal Events In The *Naval Official Records*

1 Operations of the cruisers from Jan. 10, 1861, to Dec. 31, 1862.

2 Operations of the cruisers from Jan. 1, 1863, to Mar. 31, 1864.

3 Operations of the cruisers from Apr. 1, 1864, to Dec. 30, 1865.

4 Operations in the Gulf of Mexico from Nov. 15, 1860 to June 7, 1861. Operations on the Atlantic coast from Jan. 1 to May 13, 1861. Operations on the Potomac and Rappahannock Rivers from Jan. 5 to Dec. 7, 1861.

5 Operations on the Potomac and Rappahannock Rivers from Dec. 7, 1861, to July 31, 1865. Operations of the Atlantic Blockading Suadron from Apr. 4 to July 15, 1861.

6 Operations of the Atlantic Blockading Squadron from July 16 to Oct. 29, 1861. Operations of the North Atlantic Blockading Squadron from Oct. 29, 1861 to Mar. 8, 1862.

7 Operations of the North Atlantic Blockading Squadron from Mar. 8 to Sept. 4, 1862.

8 Operations of the North Atlantic Blockading Squadron from Sept. 5, 1862, to May 4, 1863.

9 Operations of the North Atlantic Blockading Squadron from May 5, 1863, to May 5, 1864.

10 Operations of the North Atlantic Blockading Squadron from May 6 to Oct. 27, 1864.

11 Operations of the North Atlantic Squadron from Oct. 28, 1864, to Feb. 1, 1865.

12 Operations of the North Atlantic Blockading Squadron from Feb. 2 to Aug. 3, 1865. Operations of the South Atlantic Blockading Squadron from Oct. 29, 1861, to May 13, 1862.

13 Operations of the South Atlantic Blockading Squadron from May 14, 1862, to April 7, 1863.

14 Operations of the South Atlantic Blockading Squadron from April 7 to Sept. 30, 1863.

15 Operations of the South Atlantic Blockading Squadron from Oct. 1, 1863, to Sept. 30, 1864.

16 Operations of the South Atlantic Blockading Squadron from Oct. 1, 1864, to Aug. 8, 1865. Operations of the East Gulf Blockading Squadron from Feb. 22, 1862, to July 17, 1865.

17 Operations of the Gulf Blockading Squadron from Dec. 10, 1861, to Feb. 21, 1862. Operations of the East Gulf Blockading Squadron from Feb. 22, 1862, to July 17, 1865.

18 Operations of the West Gulf Blockading Squadron from Feb. 21 to July 14, 1862.

19 Operations of the West Gulf Blockading Squadron from July 15, 1862, to March 14, 1863.

20 Operations of the West Gulf Blockading Squadron from March 15 to Dec. 31, 1863.

21 Operations of the West Gulf Blockading Squadron from Jan. 1 to Dec. 31, 1864.

22 Operations of the West Gulf Blockading Squadron from Jan. 1, 1865, to Jan. 31, 1866. Operations of the Naval Forces on Western Waters from May 8, 1861, to April 11, 1862.

23 Operations of the Naval Forces, on Western Waters from April 12 to Dec. 31, 1862.

24 Operations of the Naval Forces on Western Waters from Jan. 1 to May 17, 1863.

25 Operations of the Naval Forces on Western Waters from May 18 to Feb. 20, 1864.

26 Operations of the Naval Forces on Western Waters from March 1 to Dec. 31, 1864.

27 Naval Forces on Western Waters, Jan. 1 to Sept. 6, 1865. Operations of supply vessels, 1861 to 1865.

1 *Part 1.* Statistical data of Union and Confederate ships.
Part 2. Muster rolls of Confederate Government vessels.
Part 3. Letters of marque and reprisal.
Part 4. Confederate department investigations, etc.

2 Navy department correspondence, 1861-1865.

3 Proclamations, appointments, etc., of President Davis, Feb. 12, 1861, to Jan. 26, 1865. State Department correspondence with diplomatic agents, etc.

Index

E

F

G

H

I

J

K

L

M

N

O

P

Q

R

S

T

U

V

W